BE YOUR BEST

TEAM PLAYER

. . . AND BEYOND

Lesley Gosling

Q·LEARNING

For UK orders: please contact Bookpoint Ltd, 130 Milton Park, Abingdon, Oxon OX14 4SB. Telephone: +44 (0) 1235 827720. Fax: +44 (0) 1235 400454. Lines are open 09.00–18.00, Monday to Saturday, with a 24-hour message answering service. You can also order through our website www.madaboutbooks.co.uk

British Library Cataloguing in Publication Data A catalogue record for this title is available from The British Library.

This edition, first published in UK 2003 by Hodder Headline Plc, 338 Euston Road, London NW1 3BH

Copyright © 2003 Lesley Gosling

In UK: All rights reserved. No part of this publication my be reproduced or transmitted in any form or by any means, electronic or mechanical, including photocopy, recording, or any information storage and retrieval system, without permission in writing from the publisher or under licence form the Copyright Licensing Agency Limited. Further details of such licences (for reprographic reproduction) may be obtained from the Copyright Licensing Agency Limited, of 90 Tottenham Court Road, London W1P 9HE.

Typeset by Servis Filmsetting Ltd, Manchester, England
Printed in Great Britain for Hodder & Stoughton Educational, a Division of Hodder Headline Plc, 338 Euston Road, London NW1 3BH by Cox & Wyman Ltd, Reading, Berkshire.

Impression number   10 9 8 7 6 5 4 3 2 1
Year   2007 2006 2005 2004 2003

Contents

iii

Acknowledgements

My thanks to my best teams: my courageous and loving family Chris, Clare and Edward; my visionary and energetic Q. Learning, especially my inspirational co-directors Mike Cheeseman, Richard Tyler and Karen Cove; my champions and challengers, my friends, especially those who have helped me in writing this book including Jonathan Harris, Richard Carr, Kenny Hirschhorn and Elaine van der Zeil; those who have trodden the path before me, especially Sue Knight, Peter Honey and Charles Tennant; my clients who have trusted me to work with them; and those who have guided the book and my thoughts, my 'voices' and my publisher, Katie Roden.

Series Introduction

Perhaps you have had an idea, or wanted to achieve something, but known that you not only need some skills but also help with taking the risk and doing it for real. Maybe you have thought 'it is easy for him/her but not for me . . .'

This series is written for people who haven't got the time (or money) to attend a long training course or who are not lucky enough to be managed and mentored by a star in the field in which they want to succeed. These books will be 'back pocket' resources that will inspire and give practical tips that you can read up on and use in the next few minutes. They will also help you feel confident in taking skills that you already have into new situations at work, home and the community.

Lesley Gosling
Q. Learning

Introduction: Team Player

What makes some people a team player? How can you influence others so that, as a team, you can achieve goals beyond your expectations?

This books gives you examples to aspire to — teams in big business, Big Brother, big music, big academic or big imagination. You can learn from others and enjoy the many practical case studies from real life and then think about how to apply these to your life.

This book features teams in most business sectors and also shows how their successes apply to teams in family, faith organizations, sport and everyday life. It is truly for everyone who believes that to succeed, it usually takes more than themselves.

Lesley Gosling leads the Q. Learning team of consultants and their colleagues at the hub of the business. A team that grows sales of 75% per annum and delights the shareholders as well as customers and staff. Every day, week and month of each year

Lesley is in contact with other teams in most walks of life, both as coach and facilitator.

For Lesley, it is an endless fascination how problems and difficulties can be turned into curiosity and excitement that create opportunities, results, fun and learning. She grows and flourishes and she and her team help others to do so too.

Her work takes her to different cultures, different countries and different people – some only in the ether – but the principles she teaches energize teams across all boundaries.

And her best teams are still her family (Chris, Clare and Edward), her friends and her colleagues. It is with those that she learns and laughs most.

CHAPTER 1
What If?

- Do you know how to radically change or simply improve the teams that you operate in?

- Do you know how others who create high performing teams in any context think about them?

- Do you know how you might be limiting your team(s) by your thoughts or beliefs?

THE UNDERPINNING PHILOSOPHY OF THIS BOOK

This book contains many practical tips on becoming a better team. You can dip in and out of chapters as they appeal to you. But there is also an underpinning philosophy or set of 'presuppositions' that have been captured in this first chapter. These are the presuppositions that, over and over again, we find members of successful teams holding. Presuppositions are similar to beliefs in that when you hold them you are likely to act as if they were true. Henry Ford thought this when he said, 'If you believe you can or if you believe you can't, you are probably right.'

This book holds a number of presuppositions about teamworking which include:

- 'If you can imagine it, then it is possible.'
- 'If someone else can do it, so can you.'
- 'You already have all of the resources that you need.'
- 'There is no failure only feedback.'
- 'If you always do what you've always done, you will always get what you've always got.'
- 'The thinking that successfully got you where you are now, may no longer be useful for taking you further.'

- 'There is a solution to every problem.'
- 'Conflict is the tragic consequence of unmet needs.'

Progress now

Reread these presuppositions and find out if some would be more difficult for you to hold than others. Pick one of the more difficult ones and ask yourself, 'If I were to hold this presupposition, and act as if it were true, what would I do differently tomorrow or when I next meet my team?'

Progress now

Consider people whom you know – or have heard of – whom you suspect, or know, to be in better teams than you. Faced with your situation, what advice do you think they would give you?

Each of the following sections in this chapter considers a presupposition. If you act on them as if they were true, you are likely to have more success in your teams.

WE CAN ALL BE PART OF GREAT TEAMS

Our need to be a part of a team is as strong and as healthy as our need to be an individual. Some people play one side of this paradox more strongly than others, but only the hermit has given up being a team player altogether. From the moment we are born, we learn how to be with others, and what our worth and role are as parts of the whole. And, indeed, many people dream of being part of a truly great team.

Progress now

If you want to be your best team, it is useful to spend time thinking and daydreaming about what you really want. The clearer that you become on what a 'better team' means for you in your situation, the more likely you are to create it. (In Chapter 3 we will teach you how to get clear on what you want so that it becomes compelling both for yourself and others – but you can start now.)

YOUR IDEA OF SUCCESS CAN DEVELOP AND GROW

You may already know the changes that you want to make to the team(s) in your life, in which case you may wish to dip into this book and hunt down the techniques that will help you. Under the 'hows' you will find either ways to take 'no action' other than to feel OK about the situation, or actions to change the way you behave, the language you use or the intentions that you have. In each case, when you change something – however small – you will be surprised at the knock-on effect that it will have.

Progress now

Think about a feeling that you have which triggers the thought 'here we go again!' What do you typically do next? What could you do instead? What stops you trying it? Remember the Nike slogan and ask yourself, 'Is it time to **just do it**?'

EVEN A GREAT TEAM CAN BE A BETTER TEAM

We define **your best team** as not only one that achieves its purpose but also one that meets all the stakeholders' (or 'interested parties') needs. We are not concerned with the size of a team. A team can be a whole organization, a group of a few people or, in certain circumstances, just you working in a wholly focused way.

Even a great team can be a better team. Some examples of this might be: the members can learn to be even more aware of each others' strengths and play to them and therefore meet a need for self-improvement; the marketing people can come up with novel ways of creating commercial interest, meeting a need of the shareholders for high-value shares; the manager can find original ways of looking after the partners of the team members who themselves may feel the stresses of being a 'part' of the whole team, thereby meeting human needs.

We also believe that if a team fails to meet the needs of the various stakeholders in the team, then there is a probability that there will be considerable conflict. This conflict may be experienced as violent reactions, bickering, game-playing, politics, frequent sickness or straightforward non-cooperation. **Your best team** is therefore one that invests in finding out people's aspirations and needs, and explores creative ways of meeting them.

At Q.Learning we enjoy being creative and working with people in fast-growing organizations that make a difference to the way people do business. We believe that we deliver quality in all that we do.

Part of this quality, that we recognize some of our clients want from us, is an ability to rapidly turn out detailed proposals with references, policies and evidence of a sound track record and yet also to look fresh and stimulating. Especially in our start-up years, this kind of client need put an enormous burden (both in terms of time and energy) on our small company and we were tempted to turn down such opportunities. Had we done so, we would have missed out on growth.

Instead, we determined to find ways of writing these proposals that would make the job easier and fun for us but meet client needs too. We devoted a week of each and every consultant in Q.Learning to this, when we postponed all other business. We then worked as a team to produce every possible template that we could dream up (e.g. a policy on paternity leave, quotes from reference sites on our flexibility, and how our individual responsibilities related to managing a large project). To our surprise, we had fun doing this mammoth task, mainly because of the novelty of being in the office together, which enabled us to bounce ideas around, and being able to concentrate on just one thing for a week. Those templates have been updated but are in use every day of our company's life and have been the arteries for access to business, particularly in the public sector.

This project met the needs of the business for growth, of clients for detailed information and external evidence of capability, and of our people for fun and creativity, coupled with easier ways of doing the work. It also fulfilled our goals of walking our talk with quality behaviours.

Progress now

Ask yourself who are the stakeholders (or interested parties) in your team. What needs do they have for your team to serve? Is your team currently serving those needs?

TEAMS NEED ACCESS TO FEEDBACK

Feedback is the ability to know whether what you are doing is working. If it is, then, as a team, you can decide if you want more of the same. If it is not working, you can decide what you will do to change that. (Chapter 5 will teach you how to obtain high quality feedback.) The more precise the feedback, the more precisely you can repeat or change your activities and behaviours. Without that feedback and flexibility, a team can easily get stuck in repeating things that do not work, but perhaps faster or with more effort/fewer resources. Teams need great vision and drive from inside, but they also need external referencing from the outside world. When this external reference is missing then organizations either continue to act in ways that become outdated or they behave in ways that are incongruent with their overall purpose.

Teams that behave in ways that are increasingly out of date

An idea that has a champion will take hold for a while. But it can also fail in three ways without continuing feedback:

- If team members who are going to implement and live the idea do not fully understand it, they will copy only that which is obvious to them, and the 'difference that makes the difference' may never become established in the team let alone beyond into the wider organization.

- If the idea does not grow and flourish, then it will become limited to its own time, it will hold back the team and it will not survive a change in outside forces.

- If the idea does not take account of the needs of the whole team and its various stakeholders, then it will only have solution-thinking in place. With solution-thinking there is insufficient awareness of the knock-on effects and so, when another team comes along that can copy the service or product, it will be easy for that second team to meet more stakeholder needs and thereby create an advantage or 'unique selling point' beyond that of the original team's.

Progress now

1 If the newspapers were to visit your team and write an article about it, what would the headline be? How idiosyncratic is your team and is that appropriate?

2 What are the rules of entry to your team and what behaviours are given recognition? How clear are stakeholders of the values that underpin your team and the behaviours that demonstrate those values?

3 What are the leaders in your market doing? Can your entire team afford to be anything less than conversant with outside influences. If all relevant information needs to be known by all team members, what information could you start sharing?

4 What reaction are you getting from stakeholders? What needs of theirs might you be ignoring? What would you prefer to do? Would it really cost you that dear?

TEAMS NEED TO KNOW HOW TO GET BETTER

This book offers you four ways to learn how to be your best team.

🕸 You can learn from your own team. However good or bad your team is, it will have better days, better moments than others. This book will teach you how to differentiate between these and to recognize what makes the difference.

🕸 You can learn from your experiences elsewhere. If you are aware that things could be 'better', then you have probably experienced what 'better' was like elsewhere. If so, this book will teach you how to tease out the approaches that you have experienced elsewhere and show you how to transfer these to your current team in a way that works.

🕸 You can learn from other teams, even from those far outside the remit of your team, to discover what is worth borrowing. Hence Chapter 2 includes voices from people in great teams talking about their experiences. In choosing to borrow from another team, you will need to take care that you borrow exactly that which you want and not incidental things.

🕸 You can use your imagination and creativity to dream up new approaches or to connect things that were previously not connected. This is the perfect way of leading the field. Again, this book will teach you how to access your creativity. As a successful entrepreneur once put it: 'the real trick is to gain hindsight faster' by using your imagination to determine the value of new ideas.

Progress now

Choose a team in a very different sphere from your own that you know is successful. What does it do really well? Could you borrow that idea either as it stands or as a metaphor for your own team?

Progress now

Return to the list of presuppositions at the start of this chapter and choose one that you will think about for the next few days. Try out behaviours that stem from acting as if it were true for you.

SUMMARY

🖎 Great teams become great by the people who have a vision of what they really want sharing their thoughts with the other players.

🖎 There are some presuppositions (or 'temporary beliefs') that great teams operate from which help them to act in effective ways.

🖎 Teams need to update and expand their vision through time.

🖎 Teams need to meet the needs of all the stakeholders for them to be successful through time.

🖎 Teams need feedback or external reference as well as their own review mechanisms and will benefit from borrowing ideas from others.

CHAPTER 2

What Could Your Best Look Like?

- Have you thought about using other teams as a role model for your team?
- Have you examined a team from another 'world' to see if it has something you could learn?
- Have you wondered if your best is possible?

MODEL OF NEUROLOGICAL LEVELS

In this chapter, you will be able to read about some excellent teams through the 'voices' of teams in different 'worlds': *Big Brother*, Orange, Imperial College and the London Symphony Orchestra. You may wish to use a structure or model to make your own meaning of what they are telling you. One such model is Robert Dilts's model of neurological levels (based on the work of Gregory Bateson's which, in turn, is in the tradition of work by

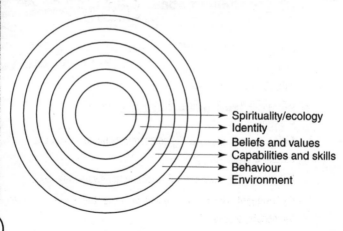

- Spirituality/ecology
- Identity
- Beliefs and values
- Capabilities and skills
- Behaviour
- Environment

Søren Kierkegaard and others). Their idea is that we operate at different levels, with some levels being more at our core and others being more readily visible to others. You could liken this to the rings of an onion.

This approach could also be represented in a hierarchical model, with 'Environment' at the base of the pyramid and 'Spirituality' at the top.

- **Spirituality/ecology**. The self as part of the universe.
- **Identity**. Who you are at the deepest level – the element that prompts you to ask, 'What am I here for?'
- **Beliefs and values**. Why you do things in the way you do? Remember, beliefs and values do not necessarily have to be believed or held long-term to change behaviours. You can substitute them with presuppositions – 'What would it be like if I *did* believe that?'
- **Capabilities and skills**. The consistent behaviours you use over time to achieve your goals.
- **Behaviour**. The things you do – the actions you engage in.
- **Environment**. The space in which we move, the where and when, the people, places, things.

BRET KAHR

From the dual worlds of television and mental health

Big Brother has been a phenomenal television success and is a Flagship production for Channel Four with an unprecedented number (for a factual television programme) of people from many different departments represented in its production. There are about 250 people involved in each year's production and yet the feeling of being part of the team is what has enticed Bret Kahr, the consultant psychotherapist, to return year after year. He returns, like so many in the '*Big Brother* village' because of the continuity of the people in the team, the integrity of the set-up and the 'nicest of people' who work in it. 'Life is too short to spend time working with people other than those who make that work enjoyable.' Bret is 'an idiosyncratic team member who has no complaints – and if I did, I would speak my mind.'

Bret is passionate about his role in psychology being to demystify mental health: he believes that everyone has troubles in their life and that these affect others around them. He wants to make the world a happier place because 'we all need idealism'. The opportunity to take part in *Big Brother*, while collaborating with 250 people who were a wider group of people than he would normally work with, was therefore unmissable as an opportunity to act as a 'tour guide to mental health'. One of his indicators of success for his role is that although, at first, other team members were deferential to him and seemed to hold stereotypical ideas about 'shrinks', as they got to know him, they learned to accept him and his temperament – his humour – and seek out his help in making sense of what they were experiencing.

And yet, when Bret was first approached with a low-key offer of a part to play in the launch of the first *Big Brother*, his reaction was one of boredom that it was just another psychological game show. He was more intrigued about being filmed at the Freud Museum, sitting in the great man's consulting room and being told that they needed 'someone like you' but in what way or how was as yet unclear.

Bret was able to discuss his role and to ensure that the protection and welfare of contestants was paramount. A 'creative dialogue' with one of the senior executive producers enabled him to form his own job specification which built upon his knowledge and experience of assessing people's psychological suitability for diverse roles – in this case their suitability for a television programme. He was able to specify safe boundaries within the production's remit, and to see the contestants over and over again if he had concerns so that he could screen out those with vulnerabilities. Bret was also able to set more boundaries for confidentiality and emotional safety both during and after the production when his role was to counsel and support. It was not just towards the contestants that Bret observed this protection and respect. There were many young women working as researchers on the production team who might not finish working until the early hours of the morning. There were always cars to take them home or to hotels. For Bret, these are clear examples of respectful behaviour of team members towards each other.

But what really enabled Bret to do his job was the team's sensitivity to his needs. The long task of assessing around 100 would-be contestants was scheduled by the team to fit around Bret's 'day job' as Senior Research Fellow at Regent's College, London, often taking place in the evening or at weekends. His first job role was clear: the contestants chosen should not be a danger to themselves or to others. He was the 'contestants' safety blanket' but the team was 'there' for him too. They demonstrated their appreciation of him, just as he felt appreciative of them.

Underpinning the ability of this team to deliver was an administration team that Bret holds in the highest esteem. The structures and systems that they put in place were the practical back-up that enabled the safety, freedom, sensitivity and respect and they were 'unbelievably cooperative'. They understood that each team member was a fellow business and professional person who was preoccupied and 'stuck into' their job. They acted as if they were gracious hosts. And above it all were the two senior executives who enabled the team to feel as if they were part of a family.

For Bret, the opportunity to work as part of the *Big Brother* team has been extremely satisfying; it has given him challenge, achievement and enjoyment. He is quite sure that his clinical assessment tools have improved, he has pride in a job well done that he has done to the best of his abilities and he has worked with 'the nicest of people'. At a practical level, on the back of his work with the *Big Brother* team he has had a huge number of invitations to 'demystify psychology' (where his passion lies) in other television programmes. He is a man 'with no complaints'! He also believes that the elements that made the *Big Brother* team so successful are wholly transferable to teams in other contexts.

Summary

◊ Bret's purpose as a team member is to make the world a happier place through the demystification of psychology and by being a 'safety blanket'.

◊ He sees himself as an idiosyncratic team member (part of a family) and a 'tour guide to mental health'.

◊ He believes in freedom to be who you are and to get 'stuck into your job'.

◊ He values safety, continuity, respect, sensitivity, graciousness and appreciation between team members – and the practical back-up to make that a reality.

◊ He clarifies his role and professional boundaries before he starts working and chooses to work with 'the nicest of people'.

◊ He learns as he works, transferring skills from one area to another.

◊ He communicates face-to-face in creative dialogues, over the phone and takes notes, using metaphors to create feelings and engagement.

◊ He makes sure he is in the right place at the right time, revelling in administrative back-up, and enjoys a sense of occasion.

◊ He uses space to create environments that are safe to work in.

DR TIDU MAINI

From the dual worlds of big business and academia

Dr Tidu Maini used to be vice-president of one of the largest and most successful companies in the world, Schlumberger Sema. Then he met a man who needed help to ensure that his university, already renowned for academic excellence, had the infrastructure in place to compete successfully on the world stage: with Harvard and MIT. This man, Sir Richard Sykes, Rector of Imperial College, London, has been told by consultants that he needs to raise £300–500 million. Sir Richard offered Dr Maini a team of professionals to help him and a quarter of what he was being paid at the time. Dr Tidu resolved to have the courage to do it: it was a chance to 'give back'.

Dr Tidu, now Pro Rector of Corporate and External Relations, Imperial College, London, has a resource that helps him in any circumstances: he has a team of friends who help keep him open to possibilities and without prejudices: passionate people who are good people and brilliant too in their own ways, who say what they think, who 'play by different rules' – some logical, some not – and yet share a common goal of the well-being of himself and the circle of friends. With these friends, Tidu is always sure that, if he needs to, he can lean on someone. He is quite clear: 'I started by being lucky: I had a wonderful family. I wasn't spoilt but they were always there if I needed them. I somehow took on the belief that I'll make it, no matter what I do.' People in his team of friends include the biggest names in world politics, music, sport, academia and business. Tidu's PDA has the personal telephone number of Bill Gates and Nelson Mandela. The variety of cultural background is very important to him to give different short-term and long-term views: the West has a need for instant recognition, whereas the East takes a longer-term view.

Tidu's way of life is inclusive. He is gracious in his welcome to all. If he can put two people in touch with each other, then he is delighted: he has the satisfaction of seeing a good result and the belief that the good that is done will come back to him sometime. This enjoyment in creating relationships is the mindset that he looks for in choosing his work-team: 'They must have an enjoyment of doing something for someone. It is something human and emotional. You might attract good people by a brand but they will only stay if they can share a work ethic of giving more than taking.'

'This choice of first-rate people is as important as processes and systems in making teams and organizations work. And strategy is the least important. You need a broad outline of where you are going and the processes to implement your decisions but you need to stay open to all the uncertainty and keep testing to see if the environment has changed. Everything changes very rapidly: it is all in flux. You need an antibody to deal with new viruses. This is a dynamic society. You need a very good management team and to be the best at what you are – in size, market position and customer happiness. So you have to balance strategy with flexibility.'

For Tidu, it means that you need to be honest with your team, otherwise they might think you are inconsistent. Team players must not be afraid of change or of changing and so they need to be close, respect each other's intellect and be continually making small excursions into what they are ultimately aiming for.

Tidu believes in small teams to try things out. He did not take up the offer of a substantial team. He wanted 4 or 5 who could 'test the water' and enable him to 'hedge his bets'. 'Always look on the possible downside: if you go for one huge thing and it goes wrong, you are dead. It is better to have several small projects on the go at once.' These projects all need to fit together in one brand, one big team, one vision. Tidu shares the vision that for Imperial College to stay at the top of university rankings and to raise its game still further, the whole entity needs to be attractive:

there needs to be a collegiate feeling: a great place to be where people are warm to each other, where there is money in the bank for salaries; where the infrastructure enables quality knowledge sharing; and where Nobel prizes are won.

Tidu says that it is going well so far but that culture change is not easy. He believes in everyone having between four and six simple objectives that challenge: each person needs to say what he or she wants to achieve in their work-life. 'I keep looking to see if my team are turned on: if not, something is wrong. But it is hard in the UK because people are so low-key or understated. You have to spot a sparkle, some humour or whether they are generating new ideas. You also have to weed out perhaps 10% of people every year to get new talent in. This has to be done by encouraging people to see that they are in the wrong job, that they don't fit and that they would do better elsewhere.'

This congruence of vision, people, systems and environment is crucial. 'Dingy offices don't work. You need a creative place that is not posh but is clean and beautiful to lift the spirit. If it is not pleasing aesthetically, then it is difficult to function. You also need someone in the team that takes care of the human side. And there needs to be investment in the people so that, whatever they do in their job, they really understand people issues: annual reviews are too formal so you need social get-togethers as a mechanism for ambitions and worries to get communicated. You also need to be connected properly through IT, processes and systems with proper knowledge management of people's contributions, skills, experience, ambitions and potential to deliver.'

Tidu's commitment to contributing is at the core of who he is. He enjoys life and has the confidence to do something useful: he loves solving problems, business issues and difficulties, but for him balance is essential. 'There needs to be a recognition of obligations to one's own life, wife, family and to society in general. There have been periods when I've been involved in big mergers where I have spent week after week in the artificial life of living out of suitcases, but then something triggers me to stop, an inbuilt set of rules that means I change my lifestyle. It is important to spend time rewiring your brain. Your brain doesn't connect properly when you are pushing yourself, multitasking and rushing to different places. You need to find an isolated hideaway with tranquility and natural beauty where you can think things through in a deeper way.'

Summary

- Tidu's purpose with his team is to solve problems and to do something useful or 'to give back'.

- He sees himself as someone who enjoys life and is part of a team of friends.

- He believes in the need for overall balance in work and home life, strategy and flexibility, task and human contact, of sticking his neck out but also in putting in sound systems and processes and in blending the best of eastern and western cultures.

- He has an outline of what he wants before he starts and chooses brilliant team players who want to give, more than take, by creating links between people.

- He shakes hands carefully, communicates face-to-face, by phone and by email, and has an enviable network.

- He multitasks but also has time to relax by seeking out natural beauty and tranquility; he listens to his internal rules that direct his attention.

- He surrounds himself with beauty and important memories in order to function well.

KENNY HIRSCHHORN

From the dual worlds of imagination and communications

Orange is one of the strongest brands around, renowned for its imaginative approach which means judging ideas by the question, 'But is it Orange?' Orange recognized that focus and commitment to total customer satisfaction and remaining true to its brand values was its way of differentiating itself in the market. It is a useful presupposition that a 'brand is only as strong as the people working with it' and so our third voice to guide us in our search for your best team is taken from those who explore 'what happens *after* what happens next?' in Orange and its industry.

Kenny Hirschhorn, an independently wealthy man, had 'retired' from Motorola aged 41 and was enjoying the West Coast lifestyle of his native USA. A call from his old friend and colleague Hans Snook, CEO of Orange, inviting him to be part of Orange, changed all that. In 1997, 25% of the UK population owned a mobile phone; at the onset of 2002 when Kenny left Orange, that figure had risen to 70%. Wirefree™ Personal Communications was the place to be at the turn of the millennium and Hans knew it. Hans wanted Kenny to help him to develop and articulate the Orange Wirefree™ Future Vision and to build an unprecedented strategy team to help pilot the corporation. As Executive Vice

President of Strategy, Imagineering and Futurology, Kenny could do anything he wanted within that remit. For Kenny, if you want people to feel different, then start by calling them something different. Internally to Orange, his team was known as MIB – Managing Integrated Businesses.

He started by observing, with a SWOT analysis (filtering for strengths, weaknesses, opportunities and threats) in his head. He then formed his team. He knew what it would look like. He had inherited two people from strategic planning (finance) who were metamorphosed into 'visionary planners', the first 'slice' of the whole – an essential left-brain, quantifiable activity. But from the very beginning, Kenny wanted to practise 'benevolent manipulation' in Orange: creating bidirectional links – both delivering messages from the central strategy team, yet pulling and cross-pollinating ideas and innovation from the far-flung operational businesses around the world. His second slice was therefore qualifiable right-brain thinking: a group of 'ambassadors of strategy' who would travel to, or live inside, the business, existing at the whim of those businesses, to share the philosophies, concepts and ideas of the corporate strategy; to listen, learn and capture best practices and innovation; and to spread those ideas among all other business groups around the world. For these, Kenny needed brilliant minds that could think in the Orange way, understand where Orange was going and keep away from acting out of ego. These ambassadors were to seek alignment of thought, a 'collective virtuosity', so that 30,000 Orange employees could understand and contribute to the vision, so that collective Orange could be greater than the sum of its parts. Kenny calls it 'syzygy', an astronomical term meaning a rare alignment of three or more planets.

This balance of right-brain and left-brain thinking was key in Kenny's selection of his team. He holds the belief that a successful and sustainable team needs to overcome the conflict between linear knowledge of process, and random intuitive 'adhocracy'. While the 'visionary planners' completed the conventional business plans needed to fulfil fiduciary obligations, working with the other MIB teams they simultaneously established the 'virtual plan': 'a living and breathing ad hoc plan that floats in space. One that pulsates and adjusts day by day to conditions of the changing world, affected by the unimagined; market spikes, technological developments, or even September 11th, 2001'.

There are other slices of the MIB strategic pie: Techneurologists who attempt to understand the fusion between what humans want and need, and what possible solutions technology can provide. There are also the Knowledge Consuls who organize the think-tanks and capture vital output, and organize random thought into the logic within the ether; the Directors of Syzygy who ensure everything runs on time, in time, ignoring time; Futurologists who seek to understand 'what happens *after* what happens next'; plus various Imagineers, Heads of Creaticity and Neural Network Strategists.

Strategy, for Kenny, is very simple: ask 'where are you going?' (point A), ask 'where do you want to get to?' (point B). Decide how to get from A to B. His strategy team was the Brain Trust of Orange. Originally, Kenny was the 'barometer' for the team. He could get his team together and talk to them. But, as time went on, Orange grew, and his 'team' became more global and unwieldy for 'hands on'. Kenny created a hierarchy with processes and disciplines that were designed to aid 'mind-melding'. He would not tolerate emails for communication: for mind-melding it was face-to-face, voicemails, conference calls or not at all. At 8.30 a.m. GMT on every Monday, his team would dial into a conference call wherever they were in the world. Each would deliver a two-minute update of what was happening in their area. 'Bidirectional communication is the key to mind-melding'.

Creating the right environment to work in was an essential for the team. While the Visionary Planners had pleasant but conventional offices, the Futurologists, Techneurologists, Consuls, Imagineers, etc., all worked in the OrangeImaginarium™. There was no isolation; they 'lived together'. Imagine walking into a space with water lights bubbling at the entrance creating the sound of a waterfall (which triggers right-brain thought). There are curves of seats, plasma screens, whiteboards or pillars painted with blackboard paint for you to write on. Toys lie around. Some MIBs have laptops on the large round table, each jacked-into one another. Others can wander out into the garden in the London square or to the restaurant, train station, airport or far-flung beach a thousand miles away. There are no files – as the Knowledge Consuls ensure that everything is in the ether, fulfilling Nicholas Negroponte's vision for a society of bytes, not atoms.

Kenny's MIB team helped take Orange through a growth that few companies will ever know. They helped to teach people that 'you are either an agent of change . . . or a victim of it'. In 1998, Orange was 5000 people (small) and 'quite fluffy but definitely entrepreneurial'. Through an unprecedented series of sales, acquisitions, and hostile takeovers, inside one year, Orange had four masters: Chinese, German, English and French, and it had to cope with 'mutating genes'. The task was to ensure that Orange would morph into a hybrid, fusing all the best traits of the merged entities. Kenny's MIB team rallied to the challenge of becoming 'the department of common sense', functioning in 'high octane mode on "90% wisdom and 10% knowledge".' He believes that teams need leaders who know how to pull people together. These traits are innate to almost everyone. Whereas some may act instinctively, others may require periodic honing. Regardless, these attributes can be learned.

Summary

◎ Kenny's purpose with his team is 'benevolent manipulation' to make a difference in the world.

◎ He sees himself as a team leader having fun.

◎ He believes in the challenge of coping with the conflict between process and intuition, planning and 'adhocracy'.

◎ He sees what he wants before he starts working and chooses bright, young minds who understand the vision and can create links between the centre and the silos, and across silos.

◎ He communicates face-to-face or by voicemails and uses metaphors and job titles to create feelings.

◎ He has regular bouts of time to clear the brain to enable him to be sure he is in the right place at the right time; he listens to his internal voices to direct his efforts.

◎ He plays with space to create environments that fit the work.

CLIVE GILLINSON

From the dual worlds of music and business

It was by chance that Clive Gillinson became managing director of the London Symphony Orchestra (LSO). In 1984, the LSO was technically bankrupt. Being one of five symphony orchestras in London means that competition is fierce, even when the quality of music is high. And what exactly was happening in the financial management of the LSO is now a mystery, as there was no proper management information, no detailed financial reporting and therefore no basis for analysis by an incoming MD. But Clive may not have reaped the full benefit from such information even if it had been available, because his background was as a talented cellist in the orchestra and a caring problem-solver as a director – with no financial or management training. Fortunately for him, 'Intuition is everything.'

As a teenager, Clive read maths at university for one year but knew that it was music that would be his future. It was later that the mathematical and analytical training (along with a great deal of common sense) helped him to set up financial systems when he moved away from playing music to take over the management of the LSO – which he did when no one else was appointed in response to advertisements. The LSO is owned by those who work there, and there was a culture of taking from it what you could. Clive faced the job of financial recovery and culture change without the knowledge of how that should be done.

Clive can reflect on what he learned in the early years: that if you never run out of energy then you will outlast any negativity; that if you have to be persuaded then you have not been grabbed by an idea and it is not right; and that people love to work for the right values in an organization.

Clive is passionate about the culture of the LSO. Music comes first: making music, making it accessible to all, being world class, playing with it and making it pay so that more can be done. He has the ideas and he makes them happen – everything is based on instinct, even pricing. And when an idea works, everyone who was a part of that initiative feels good about it. It is one of the core rules of the culture: 'We sit down with our partners and we may know that we have the upper hand, but we talk it through to make sure that they are happy too. Sometimes it may cost us more in the short term, but there will always be a long-term gain. These people are family and we always help and support them. There is a tremendous sense of camaraderie in which people can depend on each other.' Internally, Clive has teams working on the initiatives to evolve systems that work. Often, at the beginning, no one has a clear view of all the implications, so it is crucial that people develop ideas together, to get buy-in and to map out who will do what.

Doing things absolutely right is one of Clive's core values. He believes that people want to buy into a positive culture – that it is part of human nature that people want to bring out the best of themselves. In the beginning of his time as MD, Clive had a great many battles in which he invested in the LSO rather than in short-term staff benefits. For him, the music had to come first so that it built a virtuous circle in which great people attracted others like them. Some people who did not want to join in left, but it was rare that people had to be sacked. It was his biggest single task to change the culture at the right pace – and never to run out of that energy. He has a clear-cut, practical and idealistic vision with a clear and logical strategy for delivering it. He believes in the LSO and that belief gives him energy. He loves what he is doing.

This energy spills over into all aspects of Clive's life. At work, his aspirations mean that more revenue will be generated which maintains the pace of innovation, change and the demands for creating world-class music. He believes that his best ideas come to him when he is out running at weekends.

Summary

- Clive's purpose is to make world-class music accessible to all.

- He is an innovator and owner of the pace of change for a diverse team or 'family'.

- He believes in the highest quality, getting things absolutely right, 'buy-in', partnership, family, support and help.

- He gets things done by intuition and being grabbed by an idea, by knowing what is right in his bones but accepting external acknowledgement. He uses common sense, logic, analysis and sitting down to collaborate with people to become clear on the what, the how and who is responsible.

- His common behaviours include meeting people face-to-face, excitement and running.

- His environment is busy, frantic but with clear boundaries for the rest of his life.

THE VOICES AS A MODEL OF NEUROLOGICAL LEVELS

Progress now

Starting at one of the deeper/higher levels of the neurological model, take one of these voices' beliefs and try it out for yourself – how about 'Freedom to be who you are is important'? Even if you don't believe this is true, take the presupposition, act as if it were true and see what difference it makes to your capabilities, skills and behaviours. Try the same approach to 'Work and life balance is essential'.

You have had some opportunities to think about borrowing from the voices ideas that are possible through understanding the onion layers or 'neurological levels'. The model is simply a way to structure experience. Once experience has a structure, you can change it. You can select bits you need to suit your goals – with the cooperation of the unconscious mind. The higher up the levels (i.e. closer to the core) you make changes, the greater and more lasting are the effects at other levels. In this way you can change some of your age-old beliefs and some of the identity statements you unconsciously make about yourself. Those that are limiting you can be challenged and more liberating ones substituted.

Progress now

If you still need convincing that well-used behaviours can never be changed, think about which foot you put first into your shoes when you get up each morning. Chances are that it is the same foot every day – a behaviour you have adopted since childhood. Tomorrow – change it. You will have changed the habit of a lifetime!

Think about some of the team situations in which you can use your knowledge of the neurological levels to carry people along with you:

- Meetings
- Problem-solving with other team members
- Delegation
- Conflict resolution
- Dealing with customers
- Doing what you think is right

SUMMARY

- You can borrow success from other people.

- The voices share many of the same ideas about their personal missions, identities, beliefs and values, strategies and capabilities, behaviours and environment. These help them to be extraordinary team players. If you adopt them, they could help you too.

- In operating as a team player, it is helpful to think through why you do what you do – if your beliefs about yourself are limiting you, try on a new belief and then see what new advice you can give yourself.

- It is not possible to operate only at one neurological level: therefore consider the messages that your environment, your behaviours and your plans are unconsciously giving to others. If they align with your stated purpose and values then your own congruence will give a powerful message to others that is likely to inspire commitment. Complex messages do not work, simple ones do: it is therefore best to behave with integrity.

CHAPTER 3
What Do You Really Want?

◊ Do you know what sort of team you really want?

◊ Do you know how to describe what you want it to be in the future?

◊ Do you know how to become free from negativity and cynicism?

START DREAMING: THE THEORY

Just like other team processes and practices, there are 'best practices' for dreaming (you might prefer the terms visioning, setting direction, calling the tune or describing your desired future goal).

Many people know exactly what they want, even when it is the first time they want it, **and** they consistently achieve it. Each will have a different field of expertise and some very different actions, but what they have in common is a winning process for thinking about what they want. Neurolinguistic programming (NLP) teaches the thinking that has enabled this process to be distilled into a number of characteristics or conditions so that we can borrow this winning way of thinking from successful people. This process is known as creating a 'well-formed outcome'. Creating a well-formed outcome will help you to be pleased with the result more often even in new situations.

Well-formed outcome thinking

This technique is about how to dream dreams and make them compelling to yourself and others. It could be described variously as a sense of direction, having a goal or calling the tune.

When you think about what you would like to happen, you may find that you start from either:

🔊 Dreaming about the future – you can imagine having the end product and you feel proud and excited. This is proactive or outcome thinking about what you desire; it uses 'moving towards' language, or

🔊 Feeling annoyed about what is happening to you, telling yourself that it is not working for you any more and seeing that what you had hoped for has not materialized. You can imagine telling people what you think of them, shocking them by showing them what a fool they have been. This is problem or reactive thinking about what you want to move away from in the present.

What you think about has a chance of being reflected in your life. The first type of thinking is likely to focus your energy on achievement, the second thinking is likely to send you off up many wrong alleys.

Here are some conditions for well-formed outcomes. If you can answer all the questions positively, then the goal is likely to be compelling for you – and that will convey itself to others.

- What is the positive outcome that you want?
    - Is it expressed in 'moving towards' language not 'moving away'?
    - What do you want instead of the problem?

- Is the outcome self-maintained, i.e. within your personal control?
    - If it is dependent on someone/something outside of your influence, you may need to identify an interim outcome that would generate that influence or control – or give it up.

- In what context would you know that you had got it?
    - Where, when and with whom?
    - Do you want this in other situations?

- How would you know that you had got it?

  Put yourself into the future as if you had achieved it:
    - What do you see, hear, feel?
    - What does an outside observer notice as evidence?

🕸 What is important to you about achieving this outcome?

- What is the real problem or issue?
- How is your present state useful to you?
- Is the reward for the achievement of the outcome big enough to compensate you for this loss?

🕸 Is the outcome representative of who you are and who you want to be?

- Is it worth what it takes to get it?
- What resources do you need, both physically and mentally?

🕸 What action steps can you commit to?

- Especially the first step?
- And what will help you maintain it?

START DREAMING: DOING IT RIGHT NOW!

You may want to speak these next few paragraphs onto a tape so that you can hear them and allow yourself just to think and dream. You can push the pause button when you want more time. Alternatively, a friend might help by reading it out loud, while being sensitive to the pace you want to go at. (You can also use similar words with whole teams at once.) Later, you may want to write down your thoughts and dreams, with the date.

As you go through, remember that if you distract yourself with negative thoughts i.e. what you do not want, then just push those thoughts away and come back on track by focusing on what you do want.

> Now that you have taken a few minutes to clear your mind of your doubts and worries, you are ready to have a go at envisaging what you want your team to be like.
>
> You may like to take yourself into the future, not too far but just far enough that it will give you the space to be creative. And in this creative space, you are able to be part of a team that nourishes you and allows you to do what you really want to in life.

Take your time to fully step into this wonderful team and to feel what it is to be part of a team that encourages you and others to achieve. Notice the kinds of people that are in the team and how they behave: take your time in noticing the little things that they do, their gestures and their facial expressions as well as some of the activities they get involved in with you and on their own. Notice the impact that their behaviour has on you and enjoy the freedom that you have to choose how you act. Notice, too, how your behaviour impacts on your team members and enjoy their reactions. Now you can start to listen carefully to the phrases that you and others are saying and to the reactions of people outside this fulfilling team.

As you stay in your team, look around you and notice your environment: the colours, the light, the stillness or movement, the space, the textures and even the layout, and how that has a positive affect on all of you. Listen to the sounds that are there: their pitch, their volume and their tone. Notice how you feel: how relaxed you are, how excited you are and even notice your temperature – how warm you are. Allow yourself to enjoy being in a place that feels comfortable.

From the environment that helps you to be the team that you want to be, you are able to notice the activities and skills that are going on behind the scenes. The team is able to do many things and you can begin to know the skills that this takes. Notice how well you and your team are able to do these.

And binding the team together is the shared views that you all have on what is important. You may not see these values right now but gradually they are becoming clearer to you. In particular, you notice that you all share a particular reason why you stay together and can perform so well.

And with this knowledge of how your team operates, you are able to enjoy being a part of the team. You notice that different team members have different parts or roles to play and you understand how important it is for you to play your part. You know that what you do has an impact on the whole performance of the team and you know what help you need and what resources you must gather in order that you can play your part. You may want to give your role a name that is fun and engages your attention.

And with the understanding of what you will achieve together also comes an understanding of how you fit into the wider world. You know that what your team brings to that wider world is enriching. You know that sometimes the wider world may not immediately understand that and that you can help them to share your goals and to find new ways of making it all work even better.

With your understanding of how you can make a difference to this wider world, you are also aware that being part of this team gives you something special that is deeply satisfying and is right for you. You may be aware that in spite of this gain, you are a little concerned that you may lose something that you have when you are not a team. This something may at first even seem something that you could be glad to lose, even if you were holding onto it. But you begin to realize that it did do something for you in a way that may even be irrational. And you realize that, although you don't need that behaviour any more, you do need what it did for you and so you begin to imagine how you can keep the goal while changing the activities or behaviours that you used to have. And you can see that this new way of achieving what you want works well for all of you, even if you are not quite sure what it is.

And, finally, you are aware that you did something important back in time that enabled you to start moving towards being part of this team that you really want and you are clear what action you have to take and what action you must continue to take so that the team becomes more real everyday. And, bringing yourself slowly back to the present, you know that in order to create the team that you want, you have a specific action to start you off and a specific action to keep you going – and in doing these you will be your best team player.

Progress now

1   Before you can convince anyone else to become a high-performing team, you need to convince yourself. Check out how clear you are on what you want. If you feel pulled in more than one direction, then recognizing that is a big step forward. In Chapter 4 we will help you to increase your commitment to and become clearer about what you want overall.

2   Continue to think about what you do want, revisit this chapter many times.

SUMMARY

🔹   There are processes for reducing negativity or cynicism in yourself. You can focus on what you do want and squeeze out any of your thinking about what you do not want.

🔹   The conditions of a well-formed outcome will help you to have hindsight sooner. Following them will help you have a fuller sense of your goal.

CHAPTER 4
Increasing Commitment

- Do you want to increase your own commitment to being part of a great team?

- Do you want to take care of any doubts that you may still have?

- Do you want to make sure that you can inspire others?

ACHIEVING A MINDSET

> Whatever you can do, or dream you can, begin it now. Boldness has genius, magic and power in it. Begin it now.
>
> GOETHE

In this chapter we will examine how you can be sure that you are fully committed and how to point all of your team in the same direction by using focused energy.

Once you have a clear idea of what you want your team to be like, it is useful to 'get it' in a shorthand way so that you can both quickly call it to mind and communicate it to others. This is sometimes referred to as a mindset. In wanting to create a great team, the challenge that you are facing is to create a shift in attention from what exists now to what you want to achieve. As long as people believe that only one thing is possible, then they will go on doing what they have always done. Once someone has a mindset of what they want or believe is possible, then they will shift into working out how it is possible, and attract others who are inspired by the idea too. If they are not clear about the goal, then they will give up and default to what is more real to them.

METAPHORS, MEMES AND BRANDS

Metaphors

Behind our language are our senses of what we really mean. Language codes these senses. Sometimes, the brain refuses to code these senses efficiently and people are said to have learning difficulties such as dyslexia.

It is a cliché that 'a picture is worth a thousand words' and, for most of us, we know that we remember more if we see something graphically than just hear about it or read about it. This can be true even if we hold that picture internally: if the picture is compelling for us it will drive our every action at an unconscious level, people will pick this up and respond to us accordingly so that our life becomes a reflection of what we have as an internal picture (or sound or feeling).

It therefore makes sense to make sure that we have an internal computation of what we want our team to be like. Assuming that we understand the basics of language, we can then choose our methods of communicating it to our stakeholders in our teams:

🔁 By our actions

🔁 By our tone of voice

🔁 By our words, choosing the type of language that we use:

- Abstract language is generalized code and hard to grasp (e.g. 'I want a team that communicates well and performs to target'), which results in others being left with either unanswered questions as to what that means or an unshared belief that you know what it means (when you probably do not).

- Sensory-specific language brands your team (e.g. 'I see my team calling each other up at the end of the day and talking about the customers they have just been with, and then talking through how they can take issues forward the next day. And I can hear our chairman saying, "Another good year".'). This language enables you to recognize when you get there and to know what you are working towards.

- Metaphors give you and others a rich and unconscious sense of what you are talking about (e.g. 'I want a team that "dances on ice together like Torvil and Dean" or one that "scores like Manchester United" '). Metaphors are by nature complex and can be unpicked in many more ways than the original intention.

When we know what we really want, our metaphors will flow. But beware: mixed metaphors indicate mixed thinking. And language really is the key to understanding what people are thinking. Therefore, if you talk in abstract language about a team that is truly functioning but then slip into your sentences phrases like 'don't put your head above the parapet too often' and 'I'd like to take him on', people will quickly pick up that your view of functioning is treating life as a war zone: so do not be surprised

Progress now

1   Ask yourself, 'What is my ideal team like?' Be clear of your metaphor and talk to people about it to gauge their reactions. Learn to rate your metaphors like a skater would be rated for technical merit and artistic impression.

2   Check your language for consistencies in the unconscious metaphors that you are using, ensuring that each phrase is like a flower in a garden, each word a colourful petal.

3   Consciously practise enriching your communication with powerful metaphors that, like warm coals, will continue to glow after you have left.

if they go into a secret service, stockpile information or resources and throw the odd hand grenade out of their shelter. They are simply sharing your world view at an unconscious level. They listened well. Some metaphors are so overworked that they wash in and out of our minds: football and war are two such ones. Unusual metaphors that are nonetheless familiar are more likely to be savoured, embellished and owned by others.

Memes

'Getting it' in a shorthand way is how language the world over has developed. We look at an object, for example a book, for the first time and say to ourselves, 'This has paper and writing, a cover and a title. Let's find out what others call it.' If others have a name for it ('book'), then we use that word and see other similar items (magazines etc.) in terms of 'book' until we are encouraged to call things by more precise words that others use, 'this example of a book is called a "journal"'. If others do not have a word for it ('book' or 'journal') then we start to coin our own phrase and, like 'viruses' or 'memes' they may catch on.

The power of the meme (and this includes advertising slogans) is that it takes hold of the mind and replicates itself by word of mouth. Indeed, so powerful is their hold that facts and logic may well be undermined by them. So, learn to use them in your favour.

A successful 'meme' tells us clearly 'what and how'. For instance, the 'Happy Birthday' tune (a meme recognized in many countries worldwide) tells us it is a birthday (what) and that we get together with people and celebrate by singing this song (how).

Progress now

Summarize **what** you mean by a great team using your own word (e.g. flock, troupe, caste, corps, regiment).

Summarize **how** you will get there with one encompassing way of doing it (e.g. buzzy, calm, balanced, productive, happy, clever).

Brands

The power of the brand is its representation of a lifestyle. For example Marlboro cigarettes represent adventure, Weetabix looks after the family, Gucci says you are successful. Buy any of these products and you are buying into a lifestyle.

Your vision of a great team could likewise benefit from its own 'brand' or consistent message and lifestyle impression. A brand can be helpful in getting your message across to people: your customers know what they are buying, whichever person they do business with in the organization, and team members understand the criteria for making appropriate decisions.

In thinking through your team brand, you might want to take into account the work of psychologist Albert Mehrabian which demonstrates the following relationships between the influences on communication.

The Content (i.e. the words alone)	7%
Vocal influences (i.e. tones, accents, stresses, pauses, intonation, rhythm, pitch)	38%
Non-verbal influences (i.e. posture, gestures, facial expressions, eye movements, muscle and skin colour changes)	55%

In summary, this research shows that 93% of our ability to influence in any communication derives from a stimulus outside of the specific words we use.

A brand is only as good as the people working with it. It is therefore crucial that your team buys into your team brand. And if people do buy into your dream team, what will they get?

Progress now

How will you brand your team? If people buy into your idea, what will they get?

Allow yourself (possibly with others) to generate a picture, tune, action, words and feeling for this. Decide which of these can vary and which will stay the same. The ones that stay the same must be easy to replicate precisely; those that vary must be different examples of the same idea.

What is the lifestyle that people need to buy into as a stakeholder in your team?

THE POWER OF ACTING 'AS IF'

Play-acting or 'acting as if' is a powerful learning tool that we underuse as adults: secondments and shadowing are the most common organizational forms. But if you really want to create a shift in how you think about something, act as if it had happened – then you will know if you really want it and you will be on the way to getting it. It takes real courage to show commitment.

Just imagining success may be enough to focus some people's energy through time, others may need a material possession as a signal that they have achieved success at one level and may now move on to the next. Many people need heroes or role models to show them the way. In choosing people, remember that you need only copy or model that bit of their behaviour that you want.

Each of us has a different 'commitment strategy' which tells us when we are committed to something. Salespeople know this and call it a 'buying process'. Each company has its own idiosyncrasies, and so does each person. Our buying process may be different across contexts but it is unlikely that you and each team player have more than two.

Progress now

Think back to a time when you became committed to something or someone. What triggered that off? How many steps in the process were there? What had to happen before you knew you were committed?

Now think of a different context and another occasion when you became committed to something or someone (if the first one was work, now try home etc.). Again, what triggered it off? How many steps in the process were there? What had to happen before you were committed?

You may be surprised at the similarity between the two processes – or you may find that you have different ways of becoming committed.

You can now use the appropriate process to increase your commitment to your team vision.

SUMMARY

🕭 Language is the key to what is going on in the mind.

🕭 Metaphors are powerful, because they connect with the pre-language or unconscious mind: so 'clean up' your metaphors and ensure that they support your team vision.

🕭 We need a 'what' and a 'how' for ideas to catch on (memes).

🕭 Brands teach us the power of adding 'look' and 'feel' to our message so that people buy into a lifestyle.

🕭 Acting 'as if' is an important learning tool for discovering if we really want our dream team and for engaging others in our dreams.

🕭 We each have a commitment strategy or 'buying process' in a given context – following it will increase our commitment to our ideal team. Our strategy may include:

- Building a picture, sound and feeling for the future
- Surrounding ourselves with symbols of our future dream
- Allowing ourselves to pretend that we know it already and talk it through
- Finding ourselves a hero or role model and copying the part of their behaviour that we want.

CHAPTER 5

Valuing What You Have Now

- Do you value what you already have?
- Do you treasure your resources?
- Do you know what you are good at and know how to increase your choices?

VALUING WHAT YOU ALREADY HAVE

Typically, we have an expectation that people should assimilate our point of view. It can seem easier to 'throw out the baby with the bath water' than to check what already exists, filtering for what is good, while still keeping an eye on what we really want.

Whole industries have been set up on the assertion that 'we know best' so that we have anomalies such as 'teaching strategies' instead of 'learning strategies', 'aggressive marketing strategies' instead of 'customer listening strategies' and 'management decisions' instead of 'staff supporting decisions'.

Where did it all start going wrong? The MD had recently left his job and the chairman found it best to put it down to a mid-life crisis. After all, the MD had been so happy when he first arrived in the job. Sales had grown between 35% and 65% each year for five years. He had such a clear vision of what he wanted and a team to die for! They were working towards Investors in People, they had enormous success in a new market and people loved working there. What could be wrong?

Back a couple of years, the company was growing at a rate to justify a new IT system. The chairman recognized the MD's competence and asked him to manage another smaller company as well. So the MD was distracted from his single focus. He worked towards the new IT system's implementation and got to know the smaller company that seemed fairly inert, not growing and not diminishing. He decided that the new company could be integrated with his other and that, with a new customer relations approach, he could start to grow it. Unfortunately, the team of administrators or 'order-takers' were simply not up to this proactive and customer-centred approach – so they had to go.

Meanwhile, the IT project was going ahead but now it needed knowledgeable resources to help with the design and implementation of the new database. In a fast-growing company, these resources were simply not available. Of course they would have been if he hadn't made those 'died-in-the-wool' administrators redundant.

With the loss of resources came a feeling of loss of control, quickly picked up on by the chairman. And now the wily chairman kept digging the knife in, 'What did the MD expect to deliver in sales in the new product line? Why was there an overspend that he didn't know about? Was that individual member of staff really up to the job?'

The MD began to feel like a piece of elastic that was overstretched and would one day snap. He planned his departure.

Progress now

Have you made an objective inventory of what you and your team already 'bring to the party'?

If there has been **any** past success then what were people able to contribute? If you have a new start-up, the individuals at least have a history.

TREASURING YOUR RESOURCES

Sometimes when we are invited to work with teams, we are able to spend time with individuals beforehand. We are often told we will meet a 'mixed bunch' of people; occasionally clients like to give us information about people – to warn us or perhaps to help us to 'see them right'. Mostly, we meet wonderful people who respond to being listened to. People often tell us things that they have never told anyone else.

Some of these people that we are 'warned about' have been stuck for quite a while within the team in a stereotyped view of who they are. Instead of being seen as people with learning potential, they are 'in a box' that the rest of the team is sitting on!

These people are undervalued. We listen to them and encourage them. We set them up to win, making sure that they know what is wanted and how they are going to tackle it. Team members need to have mutual respect and high expectations of each other if the team is to function effectively.

Progress now

Take time to start a habit of thanking your team players for who they are and what they do. With email and mobile phones, it should be possible to send a message as soon as you think of it. But only do it when you genuinely think they have done a good job etc. The more they know what you are interested in and appreciate, the more they are likely to help you get it.

Find ways to nourish your co-team members. Food and drink can symbolize that; listening is powerful too.

Grow the habit of treasuring your resources. Think back over your past to people who have contributed to where you are now or who you are. If they are still 'around', let them know you are grateful.

GIVING AND RECEIVING FEEDBACK

A characteristic of high-performing teams is that they give and receive feedback – engaging with each other and with the world beyond. The Johari's Window model shows how we may not know ourselves as well as we could. It is difficult to know the impact that we have on others without feedback. Feedback is a high quality gift that enables us to have increased choice about how we behave.

In order to become aware of the patterns we run and the effect of our behaviours on others, we need high quality feedback. Unfortunately, this is often in short supply because people may be reluctant to tell us how they perceive us. We would encourage you to give and receive feedback regardless of whether it is positive or negative.

Johari's Window

	Known to self	Unknown to self
Known to others	**The Open Arena**	**The Blind Spot**
Unknown to others	**The Hidden**	**The Unknown**

Adapted from the work of Joseph Luft and Harry Ingam, courtesy of Mark Brooks

	Known to self	Unknown to self
Known to others	**The Open Arena** This is the part of us that meets, converses and relates openly with others. In an intimate or close relationship, this pane will be fully open as we do not need to hide much of ourselves, or keep many secrets. When we relate from this pane, more of us is available for others to know	**The Blind Spot** This is the part of our selves that others see and we don't. Sometimes we fool ourselves that we are coming across or behaving in a certain way – others may see the real us, however. Important personal learning can occur if others take the trouble to give us feedback. We may become aware of things about ourselves that we need to know. Sometimes such feedback can be painful to receive and we may refuse to accept it initially. Feedback needs to be carefully and skilfully offered
Unknown to others	**The Hidden** This is the part of us that wishes to keep things hidden from others – this is not necessarily a bad thing because we need to know we can trust people before we disclose certain things about ourselves. This is known as operating from behind a facade. If we disclose something about ourselves to someone, we make this pane smaller and the Open Arena becomes correspondingly larger	**The Unknown** This part of ourselves is really our potential for the future. We don't know it's there and neither does anyone else. It is sometimes known as the unconscious. We may become aware of it when we feel vague feelings or intuitions about someone or something

The behaviours that increase the size of the Open Arena are willingness to give and receive feedback and self-disclosure

When giving feedback:

- 🕸 Maintain rapport

- 🕸 Give specific examples as soon as possible after the event

- 🕸 State in sensory-specific language what you saw or heard

- 🕸 Acknowledge that feedback is always subjective – it comes from your own 'map of the world'

- 🕸 Give opportunities for the receiver to seek clarification

- 🕸 Often people prefer feedback one-to-one – check this out

- 🕸 Check: ask yourself 'Why am I giving this feedback'? The only valid answer is: to give information about your perception to the other person to increase their awareness of the effect they have on others. It is up to them if they choose to change

- 🕸 Feedback that is requested is likely to be the most useful to the receiver.

When receiving feedback:

- 🕸 Remember:

    There is no failure – only feedback

    Feedback is data

- 🕸 You do not have to: Defend, Blame, Placate, Justify, or Explain.

Progress now

Choose people who might give you a different 'view of the world'.

Plan what feedback you would like. Remember, 'there is no failure, only feedback'. The feedback will tell you the extent to which you are meeting the other person's needs, not necessarily the extent to which you are achieving your objectives.

Do some rapport building and ask for feedback. When you receive it, say thank you.

Use the feedback as data. What does it tell you about the other person's needs? How do you normally respond to people with those needs? Can you generate some alternative actions yourself, or can the other person suggest what they would like from you?

WHEN ASKING FOR FEEDBACK IS NOT AN OPTION

Sometimes we may believe that asking for feedback is inappropriate and yet knowing our impact on others is still important if we wish to develop our choices. Fortunately, other people are giving us feedback all the time, if we only know how to understand it. Collecting this data is stage one and is called 'sensory acuity', doing something about it is stage two and is called 'flexibility'.

Stage one: sensory acuity – noticing what your experience is telling you

Every team thinks it is 'normal'. Sometimes people ask us, 'Does every team react like us?', but usually people are insufficiently curious or will have decided what 'other people are like'. We find that each team is unique, setting up its own norms, standards, myths and behaviour patterns. From outside, these may seem extraordinary but, inside, people learn to adapt to the 'team culture'.

One of your most powerful guides to the feedback you are receiving is your feelings. When you experience strong feelings, you are probably experiencing a challenge to how you are engaging with the world. For example, imagine being at a meeting and volunteering an idea that is immediately ignored as the discussion moves on. An immediate reaction may be to feel annoyed at the other people's lack of sensitivity to you. But what if you took their behaviour as helpful feedback to you? Instead, you may then feel annoyed at yourself for having mistimed your contribution: powerful feedback to work on your timing of ideas. Or you may feel cross that someone belittled you: powerful feedback for you at a beliefs or identity level – you may like to challenge yourself as to how you came to allow someone to belittle you.

Stage two: the inner team – create change through yourself

Bill Beswick, assistant manager to Middlesbrough Football Club, in his book *Focused for Soccer* talks about 'the mind being the athlete and the body merely the means'. He challenges every team member to subject themselves to six key questions:

1   Is the player living the correct lifestyle?
2   Is the player physically capable?
3   Is the player technically capable?
4   Is the player tactically intelligent?
5   Is the player mentally tough enough?
6   Can this player control himself emotionally?

Almost half of England's Premiership clubs now employ psychologists, presumably recognizing that emotional intelligence is important for team players. Emotional intelligence suggests some 'benevolent manipulation' of tensions and possibilities around you. If sometimes you feel angry with people in your team or scared of what might be expected of you, the technique below is for you.

Using positive intentions

🖉 When someone's behaviour impinges upon you so that you have a strong reaction, you can be sure that it is because at some time and in some way you too have behaved like that. This is true whether you have noticed someone to be kind or sly. It works all ways. So, ask yourself, 'How is that type of behaviour true about me? What positive benefit does it bring?'

🖉 When you have a representation of how that behaviour is also yours, ask yourself, 'When I choose that behaviour, what does it do for me?'

🖉 By now you may begin to realize that the feeling you have about the other person's behaviour is, at least in part, saying more about you than the other person. (You may also begin to feel differently about the behaviour.)

🖉 You are unlikely to be able to force the other person to change their behaviour, but you can change yours. Thinking about what your behaviour achieves for you, you will be able to generate alternatives that may work better for both you and others. When you change your behaviour you will engage the world in a different way and will therefore not get the same reaction back. A side effect is that when you again encounter this behaviour in another, it is unlikely to raise such strong feelings in you.

Progress now

Find a pair of 'clean eyes' to examine your team. If you are a new player yourself then write down what you notice as a rich source of first impressions. Otherwise, step well away from the team to record what is going on, perhaps talk it through with someone not involved. Or ask for an outsider's opinion. Collect data, do not filter it with opinions too early. Is your team culture healthy?

When you have a strong reaction to another's behaviour, check the extent to which you do that same behaviour too. Ask yourself what using that behaviour achieves for you and then look for alternative behaviours that will give you more choice. Experiment with some to see if they give you satisfactory outcomes that work for others around you too.

SUMMARY

🖎 In looking for your dream team, look carefully at what you already have that may simply be hidden under your view of it. Look for the strengths in the team and see how they can be reapplied to the new goals that you have. Tell people what you want and how to use their assets to help.

🖎 Nourish the team by celebrating success. Ask for stories of success. Look for heroes.

🖎 Everything that you experience offers feedback to you which you can use if you wish: people nodding off to sleep in your presentation = do something different. When you have negative feelings about another team player, ask yourself what you and their behaviour have in common.

CHAPTER 6

Strategies and Techniques for Getting There

- Do you know how you succeed and how dream stealers operate?
- Do you know how to modify your own and others' behaviour?
- Do you know how to borrow what you need, ask for help or increase your own resources?

THE DREAM STEALER

First we are going to explore how we fail. We fail when we choose to do something that does not satisfy us. Choosing to stay with such behaviours is like staying in our 'box'.

Reasons to stay in your box:

- Comfortable
- Known
- No risks
- Limited – Can't – Change
- Can cope with effects
- Frustrating but easier
- Can blame others
- Disempowered

Reasons to come out of your box:

- Challenging
- Learning
- New
- Fun
- Breath of fresh air
- Responsible
- Pioneering
- Warmth

Each time we choose to stay 'in the box' when we have an intuition that a new behaviour is required, we act as our own 'dream stealer'. The language of the 'dream stealer' rejects any possibility of things being better. When we steal other people's dreams we say things like, 'you can't do that' or 'you have to do this'. This chapter explores how to recognize dream stealing and to give yourself and others more choices.

MIND THE GAP

We saw in Chapter 2 how successful team players use certain winning strategies to be successful. They have learned to reduce or eliminate behaviours that hinder success and to choose behaviours that support the rewards that they want. You can learn to do this too but, as with learning any new skills, it does involve going through some 'pain' to get there and leaving the 'box' behind. In order to become really skilful, you will need to recognize that some of what you have been doing does not now work and to consciously try out new behaviours.

But the problem with any resolution to change a habit is that we first need to 'mind the gap' between the old habit or strategy and the new one that we are trying to practise. All too often, we repeat a habit even though it is not appropriate for that particular occasion.

The four stages of learning a skill

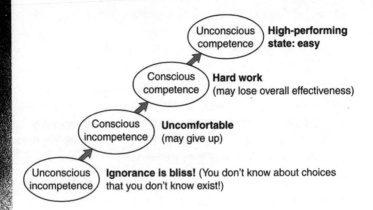

Unconscious competence — **High-performing state: easy**

Conscious competence — **Hard work** (may lose overall effectiveness)

Conscious incompetence — **Uncomfortable** (may give up)

Unconscious incompetence — **Ignorance is bliss!** (You don't know about choices that you don't know exist!)

Keith was worried about a team away day that was scheduled for the next day. Things hadn't been going so well recently in the 10 year old company, of which he was finance director. The company was used to rapid growth and quick responses. They had grown by rewarding salespeople with handsome bonuses. But, in the recent climate, this growth was threatened. The CEO had jumped ship, having kept hidden from the parent company just how worrying things were.

Keith had seen this kind of situation before and, in his view, a long-term look at the company was needed: some proper investment in systems, a careful look at the profitability of some of the branches etc. His worry was that, when he had said things like that before, he had been greeted with derision by other team members who had a 'fix it' attitude. He knew they would want to strip out the budgets and increase the sales bonuses. However, he felt that he had to say it although he believed that it might result in his being victimized and ostracized, even sacked. It was all too familiar from other companies he had been in.

Keith's habit was to act like a 'bull in a china shop'. He needed to 'mind the gap' – not ignore his integrity. He recognized that the language that team members often used was warlike (beating the competition, going into battle, needing new weapons etc.). He could see that he had been acting like a cross between their father and a policeman, rather than a comrade in arms. He decided to learn a new skill in order to tackle the situation.

The next day, he joined the group at the away day, taking care to stand like them. He said how worried he was that the company was entering a 'war zone' (lots of nods) and they'd better treat the day like a battle plan (the odd whoop of delight). They agreed to a strategy that day (a longer-term one as well as some short-term actions) and, on the way home, no less than two of his team phoned him to thank him for the real difference he'd made to the day — one even suggested continued 'undercover' meetings.

Keith had learned to 'mind the gap' and to pause before doing what he had always done before and instead choose a different route.

BEHAVIOUR MODIFICATION

In Peter Honey's book *Solving People Problems*, we can learn a model for behaviour modification that encourages us to use the gap wisely and to take control of what we can influence rather than being stuck in a loop of unproductive feelings and hindered behaviour. In this model, we can see that the outside stimulus or

How you can sabotage yourself – continually!

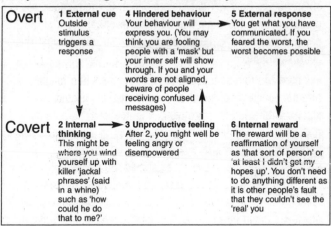

Overt	**1 External cue** Outside stimulus triggers a response	**4 Hindered behaviour** Your behaviour will express you. (You may think you are fooling people with a 'mask' but your inner self will show through. If you and your words are not aligned, beware of people receiving confused messages)	**5 External response** You get what you have communicated. If you feared the worst, the worst becomes possible
Covert	**2 Internal thinking** This might be where you wind yourself up with killer 'jackal phrases' (said in a whine) such as 'how could he do that to me?'	**3 Unproductive feeling** After 2, you might well be feeling angry or disempowered	**6 Internal reward** The reward will be a reaffirmation of yourself as 'that sort of person' or 'at least I didn't get my hopes up'. You don't need to do anything different as it is other people's fault that they couldn't see the 'real' you

'cue' is often glued together with a stream of mini events. If we can create gaps between each mini event, then we can create the potential for choice, flexibility and influence.

I once worked with a team where the team leader felt that he needed to be in control. A requirement of the wider company was that each team should be involved in setting their goals or vision. At a team away day the team members were excited about having their say but, before the start, their leader took me to one side and explained that whatever came out of the day was irrelevant as he already had a clear idea of what the goals would be.

Someone in the team suggested imagining some possible alternative scenarios for five years hence. The discussion started with a young lady saying, 'I'm not really sure about this, but . . .'. The team leader interrupted to explain how she had got her facts wrong. Everyone listened. He then explained his view of the future. Everyone listened. He asked one of the team to write down his summary. At coffee time, the team leader said to me, 'You see how it is around here: no one has any ideas about how to make things happen — I might just as well put it all in a paper and circulate it rather than go through the rest of the day.'

After coffee, we changed the rules. Each individual drew a picture of their own idea of what they wanted the team to be doing in the future. The discussion afterwards was centred on the goal of helping each individual in turn to improve his or her own idea. Certain behaviours were encouraged (seeking ideas, seeking clarification, summarizing) but some were forbidden (proposing, suggesting, disagreeing, difficulty stating) leaving some behaviours neutral (building, agreeing, giving information). The team leader caught on pretty quickly and scored more 'brownie points' than anyone else. With the rules on 'good behaviour' being clear, he became an excellent coach.

In using the model above, you can see that the team leader, believing that he had to be in control, used every opportunity to prove this belief:

Example: team leader's self-fulfilling prophecy

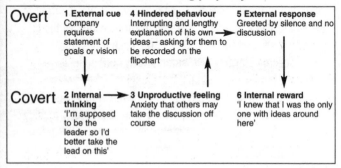

Overt	1 External cue Company requires statement of goals or vision	4 Hindered behaviour Interrupting and lengthy explanation of his own ideas – asking for them to be recorded on the flipchart	5 External response Greeted by silence and no discussion
Covert	2 Internal thinking 'I'm supposed to be the leader so I'd better take the lead on this'	3 Unproductive feeling Anxiety that others may take the discussion off course	6 Internal reward 'I knew that I was the only one with ideas around here'

In my role as team facilitator I had a number of choices as to when and how I could intervene to bring about change: and I chose some preventative ones (creating clear structure at the beginning) and some reinforcing ones (creating quality rewards at the end).

Facilitator's choices to create change

Overt

1 External cue
I could ask the team leader to leave. I could terminate discussion and seek opinions separately. I could separate people so that everyone had space. I chose to use the excuse of a change of medium (drawing) to avoid repeating the same situation and enable some individual thinking space

4 Hindered behaviour
Unproductive behaviours were ignored and new 'good behaviours' were praised. Attention was heaped on new 'star performers'

5 External response
The team members played along and had fun both contributing their ideas and developing new coaching skills. They said how well the team leader had helped the discussions and thanked him for the day

Covert

2 Internal thinking
I needed to change people's thinking from control to listening. By setting up rules on 'good behaviours', I harnessed the wish to get it right but channelled it into a coaching style

3 Unproductive feeling
I had lots of choices here: I could have encouraged team members to take action here by expressing how they felt and talking it out for themselves; or used lots of physical exercises and hoped someone else would excel in that medium; or I could have worked on individuals' assertiveness skills. By providing a clear structure, I hoped to reduce the anxiety of being off course

6 Internal reward
The team leader was encouraged to see that the 'real him' was even better than he had thought. His new choice of leadership style gave him even more power and influence

PUSH THE RIGHT BUTTONS

Stephen Covey's advice in his *Seven Habits of Highly Successful People* is to 'begin with the end in mind' – the end does justify the means. In the Behaviour Modification Model, the end is the **reward** that we experience. Knowing what 'does it for you' and what 'does it for another' is like knowing which buttons to push – and pushing the right buttons (or giving the right rewards) is vital to success.

It is worth remembering however, that everyone is unique, so each person has specific criteria for what 'does it for them' in a particular situation and only true representations or 'criteria equivalents' will do. It is worth learning what these 'criteria equivalents' are for each team member in case you violate their trust, break the team rules or 'make a withdrawal' from the relationship in any other way. If you fail to 'make deposits' in your team members' 'bank accounts' (currency for the relationship) then you may well become 'overdrawn' – and it is far harder to try to reopen an account.

GIVE YOURSELF A GOOD TALKING TO

In the Behaviour Modification Model, step 2 encourages you to put in a gap to change your internal thinking. Here you can practise playing around with the tone, pitch and volume of the internal voice that you talk to yourself with, as well as making sure that you use positive language. While you are about it, you would be well advised to play with the internal pictures you have of team activities and relationships: notice their size, any movement, whether they are framed, in colour, how clear and whether you see them 'through your own eyes or if you are disassociated, i.e. you can see yourself in them – and then alter them one by one and notice how you feel about the changes. When you find a change in the sound or pictures that has a dramatic affect on how you feel about the situation or person, then notice how that different thinking could drive different behaviours too.

Some people are overwhelmed by their work. They tend to be clever, well-intentioned people who want to make a difference to their team and the organization. So they keep taking on more and more, until one day they can't cope with any of it – and they no longer know where to turn for a way out or help.

It is at this point that kind managers notice and send them on a time management or stress awareness course and these might help. But, often, these people are fabulous at both skills – they are already coping with twice the norm. Besides, they are in crisis and do not have the time to go on a course, to make 'to do lists' or to recruit some assistance. Because *first* they need space to think.

Often when these people spend only a few minutes playing with their internal sounds or pictures, they become visibly calmer – they have been able to exercise choice where it matters. They describe their new world in terms such as, 'I'm outside our offices in a little wood. The colours are varieties of reds and golds. Through the trees, I can see the offices and I know that work is going on there but I'm outside it. I can see it going on in the distance through the windows and now I know what needs doing . . .'

A month or so later, they report significant changes in their lives – ones that they attribute to their change of thinking. These can be: planning their day so that they prepare before meetings, selecting which projects to get involved in and which to turn down, asking for more help etc. Often too they focus on dramatic events: taking up driving again after many years, arresting bulimia, contacting a family member or moving house – all of which bring about a feeling of control.

There is a model called Swish which can help you permanently change how you think about your experiences. It is particularly helpful if you are feeling daunted about an event. Here it is described as an exercise to be done in pairs with A coaching B.

Standard Swish pattern

1   Ascertain what B's unwanted or hindered behaviour or response is.

2   Coach B to create a large, bright associated image of the situation just before the unwanted behaviour begins – an associated image

will be one in which is seen directly through B's own eyes. Calibrate
(i.e. notice changes in) B's external behaviour. The image B has
created will include the **cues** that trigger the unwanted behaviour.

3   Ask B to put this image aside briefly.

4   Ask B how they would see their behaviour differently if they did not
     have the unwanted behaviour. Then ask them to create a
     disassociated image of the situation that no longer has this
     behaviour – a disassociated image is where B can see themselves
     in the situation. This is the **desired state**. Make sure it is a strong
     response and calibrate their external behaviour.

     *This is not just a picture of themselves without the behaviour, e.g.
     not smoking, rather it is a disassociated picture of them as a
     different kind of person who is more able, has more choices or
     whatever else is important to them. They may well describe these in
     metaphorical terms.*

5   Coach B to bring back the large, bright, associated image of the
     cues, and put a small, dark image of the desired state in the lower
     right-hand corner.

6   Coach B to make the desired state image get brighter and larger,
     and allow the old image of the cues to dim and become
     overwhelmed. This should be done quickly while A says 'Swish!'

Once B has this large, bright image of the desired state, ask them to clear their image from the mind (open their eyes). Then repeat the process five times.

Be sure to have a break at the end of each Swish so that the process or 'chaining' goes only one way. You are creating a direction with this pattern by changing three variables at once – size, brightness and association/disassociation. Use calibration of B's behaviour to confirm that the internal processes are moving in the desired direction.

7   Test:

(a)   Make cue image. What happens?

(b)   Behavioural test with real external cues – i.e. find out what happens in real life!

If Swish is successful, it will be difficult to hold the cue image as it will be replaced by the desired state image. Similarly, in the real situation, the real cues should chain through to the desired state image and direct new productive behaviours.

GET THE FEEL GOOD FACTOR

The third part of the Behaviour Modification Model allows you to create a gap and to choose your feelings. Your feelings are not you, they are not generated by someone else, they are simply learned responses – and the range of responses that different people might show to the same event is vast.

Eric Burns's work on transactional analysis shows that each person has a 'favourite feeling': you have become accustomed to the habit of experiencing this same feeling when you are challenged to 'get out of your box'. By contrast, imagine what it would be like to choose to feel how you wish to feel at any time. To do so, you would need to find a switch to anchor these new feelings rather than allow the same old pattern of your 'favourite' negative feelings to run again. This exercise will help.

Setting up your resourceful state

1   Think of an experience when you were particularly resourceful.

2   Imagine a circle on the floor and give the circle a colour.

3   Think of the experience now. What are you seeing? What are you hearing? What are you feeling?

4   As soon as those images, sounds and feelings begin to intensify, take a deep breath and step into your circle.

5   As you stand inside the circle intensify your experience.

6   Enjoy the feeling that is a natural part of being resourceful.

7   Step out when you are ready or if the feeling begins to diminish.

Now talk or think about something different to break out of that state; then go through the sequence again, adding a code word, sound or music as follows:

1   Re-experience your time of resourcefulness.

2   Imagine the coloured circle.

3   Say your code word or make your sound (hear your music).

4   Step into the circle.

5   Intensify the feeling – imagine the circle coming up round you like a cloak.

6   Stay in the circle for as long as you experience the resourceful state.

Remember, when you step out of the circle, to 'break your state'. If it appeals, bend down and 'fold up' the circle. 'Put it in your pocket' and practise getting it out and standing in it.

There are many variations on the sequences above, sequences that enable people to choose how they feel – and therefore how they behave – in situations that are important to them. When you have developed your own strategy, practise using it over and over again until you can be sure of it in any situation that you need it.

Progress now

Think about how you interact at team meetings, at other team events or with particular individuals. Is there a behaviour or feeling that you repeat that you would rather not? Think through the Behaviour Modification Model: notice that you do have a pattern, in which you go through the same six steps.

Now decide how you are going to give yourself more choice and take on the belief that you can choose your feelings: by avoiding the situation if possible, by giving yourself a good talking to – or changing your internal images, by stepping into a resourceful state or by changing the rewards at the end.

Rehearse the new sequence in your mind, with embellishments if necessary. Then go and do it.

SUMMARY

- To change your behaviour – or to encourage others to do so – will first require you to 'step out of your box' and be willing to try something different: this can feel challenging and even frightening: it takes great courage.

- You then need to work out what happens at each step, separating out thoughts, feelings, behaviours and responses that may have become fused over time. Be careful that you are very clear about the reward that you want.

- There are techniques for changing your internal voices or pictures so that they work with you to make you feel resourceful when you wish – or you may have your own that you are not using in this context. Practise them and use them.

- You can use the same model for openly or covertly modifying others' behaviours – 'benevolent manipulation'.

- Remember to celebrate success.

CHAPTER 7

Your Best Knowledge

- Do you know about team management?
- Do you know about the dynamics of team relationships?
- Do you know about cross-team relationships?

TEAM MANAGEMENT

General management books will tell you that as a manager you need to split your attention in four ways or 'PLOC':

- Planning
- Leading
- Organizing
- Controlling

Much of what has been covered in previous chapters is about leading your team to be your best: visions, strategies, good relationships are key – but insufficient without great processes and practices in place to underpin them. Best practices are those that are repeatable through time, transferable to different environments and scalable to allow for growth and change. So, much of this chapter is about processes, practices and systems.

Teams are unique but team development follows a well-trodden path:

Chaos → Formal → Skilful

Chaos

When groups form or reform with additional members, there is a searching for how to operate. Typically people are ultrapolite with each other or jockey for position and airspace. Often there is too much talking, ideas are offered and lost, actions agreed without consequences considered etc. Very limited success is enjoyed in the chaos stage and so frustrated do team members become that they either give up or suggest actions which move them to the next stage.

Formal

When groups have experienced the ineffectiveness of chaos, people usually start to suggest that the leader acts in certain ways, that the group adopts certain procedures and that defined communication systems are introduced. Following these can sometimes be so laborious that the group surrenders to noisy chaos, only to find it wholly unproductive and, thus, reluctantly returns to formality.

Groups often then become stuck in the formal stage, believing it to be the only way forward. However, humans are extremely ingenious and often find quick and easy ways through and round systems in order to achieve objectives – thus moving up to the next stage, becoming a team.

Skilful

Skilful teams are effective, efficient and continuously improving. They review their experiences and learn from them. Self-leadership and accountability, with an eye on the bigger picture, are key competences of individuals. The team has systems and processes but knows when and how to override them to achieve goals without jeopardizing the bigger picture.

TEAM CONTRACTS FOR HIGH-PERFORMING TEAMS

To move from the formal stages, it is helpful to brainstorm what you would like to experience as 'normal behaviours' in your team. Here is a starter list for each team player to be able to:

- State expectations of self and others
- Develop and agree unequivocal contracts with others
- Foster a culture of open and honest communication
- Keep other team members informed of activities and priorities
- Involve the team in all aspects of the work, ensuring that everyone knows their role

- Give and receive feedback positively and in a timely manner
- Coach others to ensure that they can achieve their best
- Support colleagues privately and in public when they are tackling difficult issues
- Recognize and praise people's contributions and achievements
- Provide direction to the team when needed
- Delegate, while maintaining interest and involvement
- Respond and react to issues and situations to ensure an effective outcome
- Recognize individuals' feelings and how they affect team performance
- Balance individual and team objectives
- Work to get a balance of team skills and abilities, thereby encouraging diversity
- Celebrate achievement of goals

The team can begin translating this into day-to-day behaviours in order to become a high-performing team. Although the process is a 'formal one', by using the contract the team starts to become more skilful. Here is an example of part of a team's contract:

Supporting each other

🐾 When team members are overloaded, they ask others, including the team leader, for help (especially if a change in systems or processes is needed).

🐾 Each team member takes time out during each week to notice how others are behaving and to give them feedback.

🐾 Any team member can ask others for brainstorming time to enhance the quality of tasks/projects.

🐾 If a team member feels let down by another team member, they will first put themselves in the position of that other team member to experience it from their point of view before deciding what to do or say.

Reviewing the team's successes may take the form of examining each item of the contract and accompanying statements, or 'indicators of success', and asking:

🐾 What has gone well?

🐾 What has not gone so well?

🐾 What ideas for improvement are there? The top two should be taken for action.

Progress now

🕸 Ask individual team players to remember their experiences of being in teams or to think about high-performing teams, and, to write their own list of features of high-performing teams, such as 'team members feel committed to the goals'. (This could take about 10 minutes.)

🕸 Collect these features on a flipchart, number them and put them on display.

🕸 Tell each team member that they have five votes and ask them to jot down their favourites. They can give more than one vote to a favourite, if they choose (so they will each have up to five favourite features).

🕸 Record team members' votes. The aim is to find the team's top five or six features of a high-performing team.

🕸 Write each feature at the top of separate pieces of flipchart paper. Ask the team to consider each one in turn and to imagine what it will be like when the team operates in this way. They should think of specific evidence that they will be able to see, hear or feel, such as, 'each team member contributes to a decision by listening as well as explaining their views). Write each statement on the flipchart.

🕸 The five or six flipcharts are the team contract. You may suggest that all team members should sign it and agree how often they will review success and agree changes to take them towards the team being increasingly skilful.

BASIC NEEDS AT WORK

People have some basic needs that must be met if they are to perform at their best. General theories of motivation (such as Maslow's 'hierarchy of needs') explain that our needs include creature comforts, safety, belonging, power/recognition and achieving one's potential. All these needs are present in a work context too.

Basic needs at work are:

- Define for me what is expected of me.
- Opportunity is needed for me to perform.
- Feedback to me how I am doing.
- Give me help when I need it, or when you judge I do.
- Reward me for a job well done.

The final three needs have been dealt with in Chapters 4–6. The following sections will look at clarifying expectations (people's roles defined) and giving team members the opportunity to perform.

DEFINING ROLES TO CREATE OPPORTUNITY

Compare notes with your boss. What does he think you are doing here and what do others think you are doing here? Once you can agree on the givens you will be less shocked by the assumptions.

MARK H. MCCORMACK, *What They Didn't Teach You at Harvard Business School*

Having clear goals and knowing when they have achieved them acts as a reward for many people, that outweighs any material reward, and can motivate them to repeat that success in the future. It gives people a sense of achievement.

Giving people results to achieve and allowing them the freedom and the scope to achieve them in their own way develops trust, initiative and an entrepreneurial approach to work. For example, if you ask one of your team to be responsible for 'Reducing costs in plant A', and define the measures for the target that must be achieved, you clearly give them the associated responsibility and authority to achieve that. If, however, you were to direct them by giving them repeated instructions, not only do you take away their autonomy, but you also tie up your own time in overseeing those activities.

KEY RESULT AREAS

One of the most important steps in clarifying your role is to recognize that your job needs not only to be stated as results or outcomes to be achieved but also to be agreed with those who are affected by or who use those outcomes. These parts of your job can be called Key Result Areas and a team player must compare their view of them with those of other team players, staff, customers and anyone else that they affect. This establishes which Key Result Areas are *yours to manage and no one else's*. It also clarifies the appropriate measures to apply to each. Other people's requirements form the basis for your measures.

When comparing Key Result Areas, you may find any of the following situations.

Overlap

When your view of a Key Result Area overlaps someone else's idea of that Key Result Area there is confusion as to who manages what. Both are claiming responsibility for some of the same Key Result Area. There is duplication of effort that is wasteful and usually causes frustration and anger.

> The IT director knew that the IT systems in the company needed overhaul. He started to investigate the best possible one that would enable work to flow through from back office to customers.
>
> Meanwhile, the finance director was frustrated with his software capability and looked around for a cost-effective solution that would meet his needs. He found the very one and became wedded to its possibilities.
>
> At the next board meeting, discussions were heated and acrimonious.

Gap

Where there is a gap in responsibilities some bits of the business are not being managed at all. This can cause 'silo' working ('It's not my job to . . .') and represents a serious threat to the team.

Company directors often have ideas that are up-to-date or even forward looking but on the floor it is 'business as usual'; the vision and values are on the noticeboard but not in people's hearts. Because translation is not a Key Result Area that is owned by those directors or their managers, it doesn't get done. The result is usually frustration on both parts.

Ideal

Here, the edges of team players' Key Result Areas butt up against each other, without gaps and without overlap. There is a planned way of delivering Key Result Areas while ensuring that contingencies are in place. This requires discussion and agreement to ensure that people really 'get it' – and can change when the outside world changes.

Having clearly defined results that have been discussed, agreed and documented allows for objective assessment of performance and development for the future. Appraisal, whether it is everyday appraisal or the more formal event as part of a company scheme, needs to be based on a review of achievement. All too often, appraisals are the source of dispute rather than being the development tool they are meant to be. This is often because the appraising manager and the team player being appraised have different views about the job and how the team member performed in that job.

It was post September 11, 2001, and the organization was aware that it was a vulnerable target for terrorism. The management team comprised members who had responsibilities in each area: IT, facilities, finance, operations, personnel and major capital projects. From the overview of the need to keep the organization both safe and recoverable if a temporary relocation were necessary, Key Result Areas were defined, tasks planned and work begun. Three months later, the six managers agreed that it was a model for successful task management.

Example of Key Result Areas: CEO in the public service

Support culture exists	Corporate image reflects achievements
• Loyalty • Empowering • Delivery on projects • Praised • Honesty • Working well • Listened to • Critical friend • Connecting • Cross-team working • Staff understand need for the changes that are essential	• Staff are ambassadors to public • Public convinced of real quality • Council is on the side of the public and delivering for them (advocate) • Fair reputation • Able to prove consultation works
Departmental responsibilities are clear	**Processes perform**
• Connection of departments • Enable right people with flexibility to perform • Well-defined boundaries • Working for corporate interests • Managers understand their roles • Managers buy into it • Managers not 'by-passed' but make it work	• Deliver • Individuals treated fairly • Public is heard • Properly scrutinized

Vision is understood	Member leadership buy-in
• Successful • Appreciated • Recognized by members and community • Improvement in substance (quality) and image • Identity exists in transaction, service and image • Make a difference	• Support for CEO • Buy into vision • Prepared to articulate vision • Supporting excellence and officer activity
Management team is effective	**Seamless service**
• Variety of talents • Confidence to be outspoken • Can receive feedback, open and frank • Buy into common vision • Genuine team	• Crisis management • Figurehead/backstop • Irate public turned around to belief that council has listened • Conflicts resolved

ESTABLISHING WHAT EFFECTIVENESS MEANS FOR YOU

One way of determining your Key Result Areas is to consider each of your main activities in turn and ask the question 'What for?' in order to produce a chain of results.

Here is an example for a manager of part of an Assembly process. Their main activity is at the bottom of the chain and works its way up through the 'What for?' question to the company goal at the top.

Improve the company's corporate growth	What for?
Improve the company's liquidity	What for?
Increase the hardware profit margin	What for?
Decrease factory manufacturing costs	What for?
Decrease assembly costs	What for?
Get the unit output per operator back on target	What for?
Take action to improve their efficiency	What for?
Discover why they are performing below target	What for?
Identify those operators who are performing below target	What for?
Monitor unit output per operator	

The next step is to identify at what point in that chain the authority and responsibility for action pass out of this manager's hands.

When you do your own chain, you may well find that there are some points that the chain branches out and there are a number of possible paths it could take. If there are a number of branches, follow one through, then return to the others and do the same for them.

If you do not finally arrive at a company goal, you will need to ask yourself, 'Is this activity really necessary?' Meetings often fall into this category.

Keep the chain as specific as possible. Clarify each step no matter how small. This will help you when you come to clarify the point at which your authority and responsibility stop. It will be the result below this line that is the name of your Key Result Area.

This process will give you possible names for your Key Result Areas. Once you have discussed and agreed your Key Result Areas, the next step will be to put measures against each.

Anyone who has staff reporting to them will have a Key Result Area called 'Staff effectiveness'. All managers or supervisors are responsible for their staff achieving their outputs – if you are a team leader then 'Team effectiveness' could be the name of one of your Key Result Areas.

Eventually you will arrive at a list of Key Result Areas that are yours to manage. They are the key outputs for your position. Managers typically have between five and seven Key Result Areas.

In the example, the manager drew the line for where his responsibility stopped at the point 'Decrease assembly costs'. He then needed to reword this so that it read as a result and not an activity. The eventual name of his Key Result Area was 'Assembly costs decreased'. It may seem trivial to rearrange the wording in this way but it is important when you come to apply the measures.

Progress now

🕭 Write the name of your team in the middle of a flipchart.

🕭 Ask your team to draw points out from the middle, listing all the people or groups of people who need outputs from them at the ends.

🕭 Out from these names, write down – on yellow Post-it stickers – what each person or group needs or wants from the team . . . if unsure, this is the time to check with these persons/groups.

🕭 On pink Post-it stickers, think about what team members need from each other or from external suppliers to deliver requirements.

🕭 Accountability time: make sure that each Post-it is given out to team members. (Do not tear any in half. However, it is allowable to split the deliverable using different contexts, e.g. 'advice' could be split into 'advice on X' and 'advice on Y'.)

🕭 Each team member can then use these as the basis of their Key Result Areas, e.g. 'Advice accepted on administrative support', 'Administrative systems designed and implemented'. (No more than eight each.)

MEASURING YOUR KEY RESULT AREAS

Although focusing on the Key Result Areas will give team members a sense of direction, if you go further and quantify and qualify your Key Result Areas then everyone will know exactly what is being aimed at. The value of clarifying these measures and writing them down overcomes any confusion that may exist between individuals as to what is expected of them. It also sets clear standards of performance for anyone else who takes over that role. In essence it forms the basis for a 'contract' between you and your team.

You can use indicators of success to define Key Result Areas. There are five main types of indicator:

🍃 **Quantity.** These describe how much of that result needs to be achieved.

🍃 **Quality.** These describe what the output will look like; what form it will take; what specification it must meet.

🍃 **Time.** These specify target times, duration and elapsed times.

🍃 **Cost.** These usually define within what budget the output must be achieved. They may define any other budgetary limitation.

🍃 **Behaviour.** These measure reactions: what others will be saying and/or doing that indicates successful achievement of the output.

For a Key Result Area 'Program error elimination', the indicators of success could be:

- Within two months.
- Error rate 1% (now 5%).
- Activities designed to achieve this target do not detract from other outputs of the unit.
- For all programs except those concerned with project Y.

Progress now

- Decide on the timescale for achieving your results, e.g. six months.
- For each Key Result Area, imagine stepping into that future having achieved the results. You must be seeing it through your own eyes. Notice what is happening. Listen to what people are saying. Enjoy how you and others are feeling. Take note of what is happening both in the team and beyond.
- When you have a clear experience of the future, check if you have evidence statements for quality, quantity, time, cost and behaviour. If not, revisit the desired future and take more note of what is happening.
- Write these statements down as indicators of success. Discuss them with others whom they affect to see if your pictures, sounds and feelings match theirs.

GETTING THE CONTROL INFORMATION THAT YOU NEED

Once you have defined your Key Result Areas and their associated indicators of success, it is important to ensure that you have all the information you need to measure your effectiveness. This is your responsibility for your Key Result Areas – there should be no surprises about effectiveness whenever your performance is being reviewed; you should know and have the data to support that knowledge. If you then find that one of your team members is exceeding your results in a comparable, or even a different, context, you can find out 'what the difference is that makes the difference'. You will probably learn something to your advantage.

A global corporation had just had its best year ever in spite of being in a tough and mature market. The organization has a team of product managers operating out of every continent. It has identified each person's Key Result Areas and indicators of success and these are on the intranet for all to see, comment on and give feedback on.

123

The vice-president was aware that some people were doing things in similar ways and yet were producing different results. He decided to 'model' the exceptional performers to find out what the currently invisible difference was. When this new information was brought to light, others could then borrow it for themselves and improve their performance.

In another organization, managers from two parts of the country were listening to one of the 'service provider' managers on the team talking about the significant differences in the two parts. One manager responded, 'But it is no good getting someone from your part to talk to my people because your person would not want to give away the information and mine would say that it might work there but not here.' It transpired that the rigour in identifying indicators of success had not been done and that vague measures that were open to interpretation had been imposed on the staff. These staff did now know what was expected of them and were frightened of what they might see if precise targets were set.

Progress now

For each of your indicators of success, ask yourself the question, 'Do I have this feedback already?' If so, fine. If not, you need to have a system that makes that information available to you whenever you need it. For example, if a service team is going to measure part of its effectiveness in terms of 'reduction in customer complaints', they need to have the information about customer complaints available at the intervals at which they have decided to apply the measures – possibly every month.

TEAM RELATIONSHIPS

Psychologists studying people's preferred behaviours have suggested that you can change your preferences through time but that you will have some underlying trends that continue to suit you. Teams have to connect in enough ways for them to have good relationships and therefore careful selection of who is to be in a team is a good start to getting your best team.

What to look out for

Each person has different filters: these allow you to select which data from the outside you want and, unconsciously, pay great attention to, and which to ignore. They often stay true for people whatever the context. You demonstrate them in your choice of everyday language and in your non-verbal behaviour. They are not right or wrong; rather they show how you are processing information.

WHY LANGUAGE FILTERS ARE IMPORTANT

🔄 They give us a deep understanding of a person's thinking style and what is likely to motivate them.

🔄 They enable us to build rapport by matching the person's hidden preferences.

🔄 They provide us with information that helps when influencing, negotiating, recruiting/selecting, managing performance, coaching, and building and developing teams.

If you are prepared to modify your own behaviour, you can influence another person and move towards achieving the outcome you desire. Most filters are on a continuum rather than one extreme or the other. Recognizing the pattern that another person uses will speed up the communication process and add to the clarity and understanding of the message. Your filters are unconscious and have a major influence on your perception. They create habits of thinking.

As seen in Chapter 2, team players have visions. Their words communicate these visions to their people. The right words generate commitment and passion. The wrong ones leave the people with a sense of doubt.

Another example of a filter is whether you filter for what you want to move away from or what you want to move towards (or whether you do one first and then the other). In Chapter 3 you used 'moving towards' thinking to create a well-formed outcome or team vision. If you practise using that model then you will develop your ability to flex your thinking and your filters.

IDENTIFYING FILTERS

Below is a list of filters useful in checking out differences in team players.

Types of filter	Mode of expression
Motivational directional	Towards the positive (proactive) Away from the negative (reactive)
Chunk size	Small chunk (details) Big chunk (global or generalities)
Relationship filter	Match (similarity/consensus) Mismatch (difference/confrontation)
Time	Past – Present – Future Short term – Long term
Reference	Internal – External
Activity content	Activity/Person/Place/Object/Time
Work	Options – Procedures

Types of filter	Mode of expression
Attention	Self (my, I, me)
	Other (you, his, their)
	Context (we, the company, the market)
Association	Associated – Disassociated
Perceptual position	First, second, third (mine, yours, outside)
	Judging – Perceiving
Convincement pattern	Expert – Experience
	Thinking – Feeling
Group behaviour	Task – Maintenance – People
Thinking style	Vision/Action/Logic/Emotion
Comparison	Quantitative – Qualitative

'I'm at my wits end.' He did indeed look exhausted. This was a man with enormous drive and energy who had achieved great success in the past. 'I simply cannot see how I can work with that man for another day.' 'That man' was the technical expert on whom the project depended and who had 30 years' experience of delivering just such projects. Meantime, while the war at the top flared, the project team was disappearing into silos and deadlines were being missed.

'He is completely lost in his own world. He hardly looks up at me from his laptop. If I do get his attention, then he rambles on and on. Then the next day, I get an email with an Excel spreadsheet attached which somehow I've agreed to. Can't he see what he is doing to my team? I can imagine lots of ways to get rid of him but none would cut much ice around here.'

From what you have just read, you may be able to understand that the man who was talking probably had very different filters from his technical specialist. His language tells us that he probably prefers information to be kinaesthetic and visual: 'wits end', 'lost', 'rambles', 'cut ice' are kinaesthetic clues, and 'see how', 'look at', 'looks up', 'see what', 'imagine' are visual clues. His grumbles give us a variety of snapshots which are intended to show different scenarios of the same big picture and we have no concrete information at all: this tells us that he probably has a preference both for big chunk and for options. For timeframe, nearly all of his language is based in the present, with a short-term view of about a day, i.e. 'in time'. In terms of attention, he clearly has a filter that is I, me and my.

So: visual, kinaesthetic, big chunk, options, present, short term, and I, me, my.

Where there is conflict, it is very likely that the other man has some opposite filters: auditory, detail, procedure, through time (past/present/future), long-term and context driven.

The information gleaned from the first man gives some clues about how to connect or build rapport with the man he was in conflict with. This gives choice. In this situation, you can choose to behave just as the first man had before – and probably achieve the same outcome – or behave with flexibility in line with the person with whom you wish to communicate, i.e. **Match–Pace–Lead**. Match the other's filters, keep it going as long as you need to develop rapport i.e. pace and then start leading to achieve your outcome. In essence, you are talking his language, not yours.

There are many psychological models, that give other ways of considering filters and/or 'personality types'. All of them invite you to enter the other person's world and speak their own peculiar language. Summaries of these follow.

LEARNING STYLES

Peter Honey has explored how we can identify our own learning style and the impact that this is likely to have on those around us.

We may have a preference for starting our learning from any of the following points:

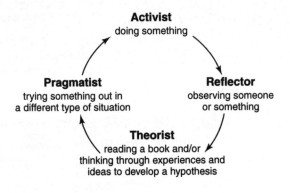

Activist
doing something

Reflector
observing someone
or something

Theorist
reading a book and/or
thinking through experiences and
ideas to develop a hypothesis

Pragmatist
trying something out in
a different type of situation

Our preference will determine our learning style (Activist, Reflector, Theorist, Pragmatist) and we will filter for activities that support that style.

It is possible to be dominated by our preference. For example, an activist may claim 'lots of experience', but he has done the same thing 100 times and learned nothing. A theorist may love reading the best ideas but never puts them into action.

Good learners therefore complete the cycle, from wherever the starting point may be. They also set up learning experiences for others based on the others' preferred starting point. This is using the power of choice through information about filters.

LEADERSHIP STYLES

Hersey and Blanchard have built on a wealth of thought since the early twentieth century that seeks to find the right filters for successful leadership. Their solution is a match between what the follower needs and what the leader is able to give. The diagram below shows a new team player's journey in self-development and how their team leader's style needs to change.

1   On arrival, the new team players are immature in their job: highly willing but not yet competent. They need to be told about their job and its context.

2   A few months in, the team players are still fairly immature: probably less willing and only moderately competent. They need to be sold on ideas about their job and its context, with time being spent convincing them.

3   A year or so in, perhaps, the team players are fairly mature in their job: moderately comfortable and willing and fairly competent. They need coaching: to be supported and listened to in order to encourage them to be continually improving.

4   After the team players have experienced all aspects of their job, they can become extremely mature in their job: highly willing and highly

competent. They do not need either much direction about their job and its context, or much leadership input: they need to feel empowered or self-motivated and to be trusted to do the best possible job – with celebration of success and support when they need it. This moves them into box 5 and true ownership.

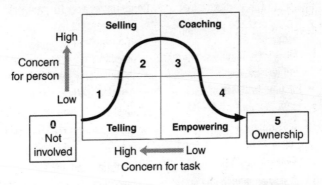

The key to using these filters is to notice when people are not where they 'should be' in each aspect of their job. Using Match–Pace–Lead you can vary your style to help them develop.

BELBIN'S TEAM ROLES

Belbin's studies with learning teams led him to the conclusion that successful teams need people for each of the team roles set out below.

Chairman (Team controller)	Company worker (Organizer)
• Makes best use of team resources • Recognizes team's strengths and weaknesses • Ensures best use of each team member's potential	• Turns concepts and plans into practical working procedures • Carries out agreed plans systematically
Plant (Source of original solutions)	Monitor-educator (Problem analyser)
• Produces new ideas and strategies, especially for major issues • Finds new ways of tackling the team's problems	• Identifies and analyses problems • Evaluates ideas and suggestions, so that the team is better placed to take balanced decisions

Resource investigator (Creative negotiator)	Team worker (Internal facilitator)
• Explores and reports on ideas, developments and resources outside the team • Finds and cultivates potentially useful outside contacts • Conducts negotiations with external contacts	• Supports other members in their strengths (e.g. builds on their ideas) • Underpins members in their shortcomings • Improves communication between team members • Fosters team spirit
Shaper (Slave-driver)	Completer-finisher (Delivery guarantor)
• Directs attention to setting objectives and establishing priorities • Seeks to impose a shape or pattern on group discussion and group output	• Ensures that team gets timings right • Ensures that team doesn't forget important things • Looks for aspects that need extra attention • Maintains a sense of urgency in the team

FIRO B

Schultz's interpersonal relationship model was first developed to answer the question, 'Which soldiers will form good combat teams when under battle conditions?' FIRO B looks at three types of filter, each with a variant, and suggests that a match of filters is likely to make for good team relations.

	Affection	Control	Intimacy
Expressed This is observable behaviour	**Expressed Inclusion** High • Outgoing • Talkative • Joining in Low • Distant • Loner • Withdrawn	**Expressed Control** High • Takes the lead • Dominates discussions/ decisions • Shapes ideas Low • Waits for others • Agrees	**Expressed Affection** High • Empathetic • Warmth • Authentic Low • Focuses on ideas or outside world • Impersonal/ objective

	Affection	Control	Intimacy
Wanted This is not observable but internally driven (problems can arise in 'congruence' and success when the top and bottom lines do not match)	**Wanted Inclusion** High • Seeks to be included • Likes invitations Low • Prefers to 'sit at home with the cat'	**Wanted Control** High • Seeks out others to decide • Asks for direction Low • Resists others taking the lead • Dislikes being told what to do	**Wanted Affection** High • Likes intimacy • Likes warm and friendly people Low • Dislikes intimacy • Sphinx-like

Using these filters will enable you to decide how to approach people. The difficulty may be that what someone does and what they want may be different.

MYERS BRIGGS TYPE INDICATOR (MBTI)

The mother and daughter team, Katharine Cook Briggs (1875–1968) and Isabel Briggs Myers (1897–1980) were horrified by how conflict could arise between people, especially on the magnitude of World War I. They started to explore filters that they perceived to be human personality differences and then refocused their work after coming across Carl Gustav Jung's ideas. They settled on four preferences, each with switches that, 'like day or night', can either be one's preference or not. These are very like some of the neurolinguistic programming filters: (I) introvert or (E) extrovert; (N) intuition or (S) sensing; (T) thinking or (F) feeling; (J) judging or (P) perceiving. They have then taken these four pairs of preferences and looked at the interplay between each one, with a resultant 16 'personality types'. The MBTI 'types' or 'filters' are set out below (pp. 142–5).

Progress now

🖎 Using any of the models below and the filters they use, think about a team member with whom you get on well. Which of the filters can you recognize?

Do the same with a team member with whom you get on less well.

Use your imagination to play around with what it would be like if those people had each other's filters – how do your reactions to them alter?

🖎 Put yourself 'into' the team member with whom you get on less well and experience the world as they do. How does your normal behaviour towards that person seem? What might be preferred?

🖎 Practise putting yourself into 'other people's shoes' and experiencing the world as they do. Sit like them, talk like them and think like them. Use this data to give yourself more choice and flexibility.

Sensing types

Introverts

ISTJ	**ISFJ**
Serious, quiet, earn success by concentration and thoroughness. Practical orderly, matter-of-fact, logical, realistic and dependable. See to it that everything is well organized. Take responsibility. Make up their own minds about what should be accomplished and work towards it steadily, regardless of protests or distractions	Quiet, friendly, responsible and conscientious. Work devotedly to meet their obligations. Lend stability to any project or group. Thorough, painstaking, accurate. Their interests are usually not technical. Can be patient with necessary details. Loyal, considerate, perceptive, concerned with how other people feel
ISTP	**ISFP**
Cool onlookers – quiet, reserved, observing and analysing life with detached curiosity and unexpected flashes of original humour. Usually interested in cause and effect, how and why mechanical things work and in organizing facts using logical principles. Excel at getting to the core of a practical problem and finding the solution	Retiring, quietly friendly, sensitive, kind, modest about their abilities. Shun disagreements, do not force their opinions or values on others. Usually do not care to lead but are often loyal followers. Often relaxed about getting things done because they enjoy the present moment and do not want to spoil it by undue haste or exertion

Intuitive types

INFJ Succeed by perseverance, originality and desire to do whatever is needed or wanted. Put their best efforts into their work. Quietly forceful, conscientious, concerned for others. Respected for their firm principles. Likely to be honoured and followed for their clear visions as to how best to serve the common good	**INTJ** Have original minds and great drive for their own ideas and purposes. Have long-range vision and quickly find meaningful patterns in external events. In fields that appeal to them, they have a fine power to organize a job and carry it through. Sceptical, critical, independent, determined, have high standards of competence and performance
INFP Quiet observers, idealistic, loyal. Important that outer life be congruent with inner values. Curious, quick to see possibilities, often serve as catalysts to implement ideas. Adaptable, flexible and accepting unless a value is threatened. Want to understand people and ways of fulfilling human potential. Little concern for possessions or surroundings	**INTP** Quiet and reserved. Especially enjoy theoretical or scientific pursuits. Like solving problems with logic and analysis. Interested mainly in ideas, with little liking for parties or small talk. Tend to have sharply defined interests. Need careers where some strong interest can be used and useful

Introverts

Sensing types

E x t r o v e r t s	**ESTP** Good at on-the-spot problem solving. Like action, enjoy whatever comes along. Tend to like mechanical things and sports, with friends on the side. Adaptable, tolerant, pragmatic; focused on getting results. Dislike long explanations. Are best with real things that can be worked, handled, taken apart, or put together	**ESFP** Outgoing, accepting, friendly, enjoy everything and make things more fun for others by their enjoyment. Like action and making things happen. Know what's going on and join in eagerly. Find remembering facts easier than mastering theories. Are best in situations that need sound common sense and practical ability with people
	ESTJ Practical, realistic, matter-of-fact, with a natural head for business or mechanics. Not interested in abstract theories; want learning to have direct and immediate application. Like to organise and run activities. Often make good administrators; are decisive, quickly move to implement decisions; take care of routine details	**ESFJ** Warm-hearted, talkative, popular, conscientious, born cooperators, active committee members. Need harmony and may be good at creating it. Always doing something nice for someone. Work best with encouragement and praise. Main interest is in things that directly and visibly affect people's lives

Intuitive types

ENFP Warmly enthusiastic, high spirited, ingenious and imaginative. Able to do almost anything that interests them. Quick with a solution for any difficulty and ready to help anyone with a problem. Often rely on their ability to improvise instead of preparing in advance. Can usually find compelling reasons for whatever they want	**ENTP** Quick, ingenious, good at many things. Stimulating company, alert, outspoken. May argue for fun on either side of a question. Resourceful in solving new and challenging problems, but may neglect routine assignments. Apt to turn to one new interest after another. Skilful in finding logical reasons for what they want
ENFJ Responsive and responsible. Feel real concern for what others think or want, and try to handle things with due regard for other people's feelings. Can present a proposal or lead a group discussion with ease and tact. Sociable, popular, sympathetic. Responsive to praise and criticism. Like to help others and enable people to achieve their potential	**ENTJ** Frank, decisive, leaders in activities. Develop and implement comprehensive systems designed to solve organizational problems. Good in anything that requires reasoning and intelligent talk, such as public speaking. Are usually well-informed and enjoy adding to their fund of knowledge

E x t r o v e r t s

CROSS TEAMWORKING

Each team has its own culture, whether or not it has defined it. These cultures may seem to be idiosyncratic but Professor Graves at Harvard University pulled together various similar threads to give you some quick and easy ways of making sense of different cultures so that you can work out how to communicate across teams. His theory is called Spiral Dynamics.

Every team or organization has two orders of challenges:

1 The Life Conditions outside (market forces, political interventions, competitor initiatives etc.).

2 The Thinking Systems inside (beliefs, values, business models etc.).

The team needs to identify the one and give direction to the other in order to integrate the demands of current working practices and of new requirements. Inevitably, this means that teams generate very different cultures as they adapt to fit in with outside demands and to adjust their inside thinking.

Spiral Dynamics identifies eight points on the spiral that have corresponding outside Life Conditions and inside Thinking Systems. Where there is a match, then the organization is at its healthiest. These are given colours to reduce the risk of suggesting any is 'right'.

🜂 **Beige.** Outside is primitive, a state of nature – inside people are concerned with basic survival needs (banding together to stay alive, automatic and instinctive).

🜂 **Purple.** Outside is mysterious and frightening – inside people placate the 'founder' (this could be the family-run organization) and gather together for safety (kinship, tribes and lucky charms are given power). There are several 'tribes' in one company.

🜂 **Red.** Outside is rough and hard like a jungle – inside people fight to survive in spite of others (egocentrically concerned with power and empires).

🜂 **Blue.** Outside is controlled by higher authorities and guilt-driven – inside people obey the rightful higher authority (and stay firmly 'inside the box', in control, with clear lines of authority and structure, enjoying stability and written procedures).

🜂 **Orange.** Outside is full of opportunities to take control (any fast growth sector will require plenty of entrepreneurial attitude) – inside people will pragmatically test options for success (and measure success in terms of achievement, materialism and a strive/drive approach).

- ❧ **Green.** Outside is the natural habitat for all humanity (many HR people would like staff well looked after and happily working in teams even if this is not seeing a pay-off in profit or service delivery) – inside people form clubs and communities to experience growth (requiring a strict conduct of consensus, community bond, harmony and equity).

- ❧ **Yellow.** Outside is a complex system at risk of collapse (leading-edge individuals and organizations challenging the big players' hold on prices or conventions in order to allow freedom of information and ideas) – inside people are learning how to be free (using integrative thinking, systemic processes, with flexible behaviours to stay 'in the flow').

- ❧ **Turquoise.** Outside is a single, living interdependent entity – inside people are seeking the order beneath earth's chaos (holistic, global and experiential).

The PR agency is in Soho and the staff wear black – what in New York is called 'downtown clothes' – but the directors wear fashionable and stylish little numbers, carefully commenting on what each other and visitors wear. The offices have charm and vitality with an air of the décor being taken from many, different, almost 'new age' styles that add creativity to the atmosphere. Yet, within these almost 'other worldly' conditions, there are signs of frenetic activity: deadlines to be met, phone calls being received, press conferences to be arranged. This is an 'orange' culture with 'turquoise' aspirations. A visiting team facilitator would need to wear a classy but one-off outfit to show that they had 'got it'.

The IT Corporation is in the City. Employees are mostly men, so white shirts and dark suits are worn. The offices have lots of glass, chrome and concrete with flashy technology. The flowers and the receptionists welcome visitors in pre-arranged style – with a printed pass at the ready. The current share price glows in red above their desk. Brochures, in red and black, tell visitors of marketing events in the next three months. The meeting room, one of several – staff work from rather noisy 'hot desks' – has a plain carpet, overlarge table for the room, telephone and chairs – with a potted plant arrangement in the corner. This is an 'orange' culture with a bit of 'red'. For the visiting team facilitator it means a flashy, dark and expensive suit and a palmtop clutched tightly: so that they know you are successful and 'leading edge' too.

TEN PRINCIPLES OF SPIRAL DYNAMICS

1   People value different things because they think in different ways.

2   Different organizations – companies and governments – occupy different positions on the Spiral and need to develop managerial/governance strategies that match their people, their visions of the future, and the jobs they perform today.

3   Managers should develop a consistent and systemic approach to all the issues within the organizational loop – recruitment, selection, placement, training, internal management, and external marketing – so they all align, integrate and synergize.

4   Organizations should be constructed from both the top down and the bottom up, to link the functions, intelligences and decision structures that the more complex problems ahead will demand.

5   Successful organizations are in danger of failing if they continue to manage people in the ways that made them successful in the first place.

6   Many people need to be managed quite differently today because they have moved on the Spiral even further and faster than most of their bosses, teachers and even parents.

7   Marketing strategies often fail because the designers use their 'marketing mirrors' and assume that the audiences they are trying to reach share their own values systems.

8   The question is not 'How do you motivate people?', but 'How do you relate what you are doing to their natural motivational flows?' A person has a right to be who they are.

9   The present issues with productivity, quality, political instability and restructuring are signs of growth and not decay which will force us to find new and innovative ways to manage people based on who they have now become.

10 Since people learn in different ways from different kinds of teachers, the task of education is to match learners, instructors, learning situations and technologies designed for fit, function and flow.

Progress now

Think about the culture or colour that best describes your team.

If you are finding that you 'fit' the outside conditions that you are operating in then your culture is healthy. If not, describe the outside conditions in terms of colour. What changes are being demanded of you and your team and how can you create a strategy for change?

Thinking about other teams that your team deals with, what colours are their cultures and how can you match their expectations of you?

SUMMARY

🜚 Your team will go through chaos and formal stages before being skilful and it may stick at any stage. Structures, systems, processes, team contracts and role clarification are part of the formality that help to underpin skilfulness.

🜚 Key Result Areas are areas of the business in which you have the discretion and freedom to bring about change and results.

🜚 Teams need leadership that can adapt to the different maturity levels of the team towards tasks.

🜚 Every team player is different and filters information in different ways. Communication therefore needs to be sensitive to these different filters or conflict can arise.

🜚 Each team develops its own culture. Teams need to check that their culture fits with the outside conditions. Communication needs to be phrased in different ways to match the needs of other teams that you are dealing with.

🜚 In influencing others, remember to enter their world and to Match–Pace–Lead using their filters or language.

CHAPTER 7: Your best knowledge

CHAPTER 8
Your Best Skills

- Do you know how to develop team cohesiveness?
- Do you know how to benefit from conflict in teams?
- Do you know how to really listen to team players?

TEAM COHESIVENESS

The onion (or 'neurological levels') model introduced in Chapter 2 (page 16) can also help you in developing what your team wants to be saying or giving out as messages to the world, and for internal cohesiveness. Teams that develop this consistently have a 'brand'. The layers of a person, team or brand can be seen like the onion.

In team terms (and organizational speak), the onion layers could be relabelled as:

- **Mission** (Spirituality/ecology) – answering the question 'what for?'
- **Team identity and name** (Identity) – answering the question 'who?'
- **Core values** (Beliefs and values) – answering the question 'why?' or 'what is important?'
- **Vision** (Capabilities and skills) – answering the question 'how?'
- **Ground rules** (Behaviour) – answering the question 'what?'
- **Context** (Environment) – answering the question 'when?' or 'where?'

When all the layers reinforce each other and are consistent, i.e. they have integrity and congruence, then the team will 'walk its talk' and have a strong brand that people both inside the team and outside will immediately recognize.

MISSION – WHAT FOR?

As with an individual and an organization, so with your team: the mission will influence all the other levels. If you are unclear about the big message, i.e. the purpose of what you are about, then your team will falter. People are more likely to get up in the morning when they know what for.

A good mission is a guide and filter for everything that goes on in the team, from recruitment to delivering to customers. It does not say how you will achieve it. Every word counts, as does the order of those words – when the going gets tough, it is often because the activities are outside the mission. Here are a couple of examples:

> Imperial College embodies and delivers world class scholarship, education and research in science, engineering and medicine, with particular regard to their application in Industry, Commerce and Healthcare. We will foster interdisciplinary working within the College and collaborate widely externally.

> Q.Learning: We are a team in business to energize organizations for them to make light work of achieving their missions. We enable every individual to play their part.

TEAM IDENTITY AND NAME – WHO ARE WE?

Any trainer will know that if they have a group of, say, 12 people and randomly these are split into two groups for a task, those two sub-groups will create a 'them and us'. Our need to 'belong' may vary from person to person but, in a very short space of time, we can nonetheless identify ourselves with others and recognize who is not 'one of us'.

In the 1980s, British Nuclear Fuels Ltd (BNFL) changed the name of its Windscale plant to Sellafield. Windscale had a very poor reputation with the public, and BNFL needed to improve both the plant's and its own image. It recognized the importance of a name, and so changed one that had negative connotations.

CORE VALUES – WHAT IS IMPORTANT TO US?

Core values are the everyday guides to knowing how successful you are as a team. They need to be the filter for every decision. These values reflect the team players' own values but, usually, newcomers will catch on and adjust. Trauma comes to teams that are forced to merge even though the values are too extreme and the common purpose not sufficiently compelling. Mergers may fail at this point, rather than because the systems need integrating.

Where team players' values overlap, a team will be strong. If there is substantial variation in beliefs and values, then you will need to manage that conflict (see below) in order to harness the energies of both parties. If you champion more than five core values, then you have a list, not a commitment, and it is unlikely that all the team will remember them.

Values are important when the going gets tough. Can you keep rolling out delivery if you value innovation? Or cut costs across the board if you value quality? It might be much easier to do either of the above, but you kill your team spirit and your brand. High-performing teams value their values and accept them as challenging.

VISION – HOW DO WE DO WHAT WE DO?

A vision is a statement of what you want your team to be like in the future as if it were here now. Famous visions include: 'I see a computer on every desk' (Bill Gates) and 'I see one nation, one people. Then I see us dealing with the economic situation' (Nelson Mandela). The real power is the way in which we make our vision so compelling that it provides our focus and sense of direction such that others can come to understand our 'reality' (for more detail, see Chapter 3).

Your team needs to have a shared understanding of how things will be different in the future and how reality will then be visible to them all.

GROUND RULES – WHAT DO WE DO?

In Chapter 7 you were encouraged to work out a team contract. These are behaviours that every team player signs up to. By thinking through the ground rules of a team contract, team players tend to feel surer of themselves and that what they are doing fits. Here are some examples from the ground rules of a management team that had experienced a lack of trust:

- Each point must 'stick'. Any points agreed as a team stay agreed until the team renegotiates them. No two-way 'collusion' by individuals – deliberate inclusion of all in team decisions.

- Each decision made needs to include thought about the customer's point of view.

- Other people outside the team can contribute to help and give advice but not to be part of the decision-making process.

- All changes agreed must be good for the community and for the team, for individuals and the department.

- Each person to be honest – if unsure, to ask for time out.

- There will be respect for each other as human beings at all time.

- Discussions will be confidential, i.e. with team members and partners and mentors only.

- The past can be talked about as long as it is relevant data for the future.

- Even tough things will be talked through – at the end, the team leader's decision will be respected.

- When a team member makes a mistake, another team member will look out for him/protect him while holding the team's best interests at heart.

CONTEXT AND ENVIRONMENT – WHEN AND WHERE?

The environment in which we operate both reinforces and leads our thinking. Each choice of décor is a coded message about what the team and the individual is saying. Each neglected, wilting plant tells a story. Each tidy desk demonstrates an attitude rather than a workload. The bigger chair, the car parking space and the desk facing away from the window are all clues. And, at least unconsciously, we are able to read them.

A change of environment is an important symbol of a change of mind; it can also lead to a change in behaviour.

The factory felt different. There were plants in the racks above the workstations. Each person was checking their own work. There were computers at each production team's hub for emailing suppliers direct about problem supplies. How very different from a year before when the antagonism between the production and quality departments had run rife.

In a moment of frustration, the production manager had ordered the wall to be knocked down. The wall had been built years before so that the quality control staff could be out of sight while they ran tests on the finished products. Since then, there had been a 'them and us' rivalry. But when the wall came down, production and quality staff had, literally, to work beside each other and so they started to talk, and talking led to improvements, and improvements led to a decision that quality should be something built into the product not just tested for at the end.

So now production staff were responsible for the final quality of a product and quality staff were responsible for dovetailing the processes and practices. The British and European quality awards started to line the walls.

Progress now

Collect your team together in a large/long room. Start with all team players gathered at one end (standing) and a facilitator/scribe at the other.

Ask the team to generate ideas about what they see as their ideal surroundings: 'Where do we imagine ourselves working?' Write each idea down on flip chart paper.

Move the team a little up the room. Ask: 'What do we imagine ourselves doing?' Keep moving, asking, writing for each of the following: 'How do we see ourselves doing what we do?', 'What is important to us?/Why do we do it?', 'Who are we?', 'What do we do it for?'

Tidy up the contributions but use the exact words that were written down to have a shared sense of the team.

Repeat this exercise annually to update the vision.

BENEFITING FROM CONFLICT

In Chapter 1 we examined how, by taking on certain beliefs (or presuppositions) as if they were temporarily true, we could benefit from the frame of mind that they gave us. Marshall Rosenberg, an international peace mediator, gives us one such belief to experiment with: 'Conflict is the tragic consequence of unmet needs.' The assumption behind this is that, if we discover and meet the needs, the conflict will be avoided or diminished. But experience also shows that it can be much better than that: it can lead to personal and team growth and an improved outcome for all.

What makes it possible to benefit from apparently conflicting needs is to avoid mistaking needs for solutions. They are not the same thing. By 'chunking up' and asking the people in disagreement, '**Why** do you want to do that?' or '**What is important** to you about doing that?' you are changing levels (or onion layers). Their answers usually reveal a host of possibilities which can be combined to project you into new solutions. By acting 'as if' that were possible, you are 'connecting things that were previously unconnected', which is a good definition of creativity or 'thinking out of the box'.

The key is to let people make decisions in their good time rather than forcing solutions upon them: recognizing that combining needs and making decisions only where necessary allows for creative collaborative outcomes.

Chunking – from conflict to collaboration

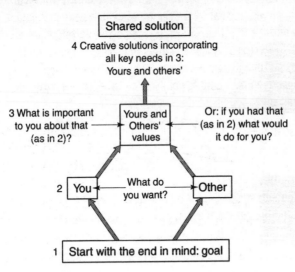

Shared solution

4 Creative solutions incorporating
all key needs in 3:
Yours and others'

3 What is important
to you about that
(as in 2)?

Yours and
Others'
values

Or: if you had that
(as in 2) what would
it do for you?

2 You   What do
you want?   Other

1 Start with the end in mind: goal

Progress now

Recall to mind the goal of being in rapport as team players and of delivering outcomes for stakeholders.

Listen to discussions, or even throwaway remarks, from your team players; repeat to the person what they have just said and add the question, 'So what is important to you about that?' (e.g. in response to, 'I don't suppose I'm going to get away on time tonight', you could say, 'You say you don't suppose you are going to get away on time tonight; what is important to you about that, specifically?')

Add your own needs — or those of another party — to that team player's needs (e.g. 'So you need to get your wife some flowers; I need to know what I'm doing tomorrow; and Sarah needs a cigarette break.')

Go 'outside the box' for solutions (e.g. 'So, what if Sarah went out and bought the flowers, while having her cigarette, and we spend the next half hour sorting out tomorrow?')

Check that the final solution meets all the needs.

LISTENING TO TEAM PLAYERS

Imagine being able to increase your range and depth of personal understanding about other team players' views so that you can see how they behave and why. This would give you more choice and flexibility in how you behave. Below is a technique to move from one perspective to another to gain different views on what is going on. Start in 'my shoes' where you are sitting. Move to another chair for 'your shoes'. Move away to where you can see both chairs for 'fly on the wall'.

'My shoes'

In 'my shoes', you see the world through your own eyes, hear it through your own ears, and get in touch with your own feelings. This can be a difficult state to maintain if, for example, you feel great sympathy for the other person. Conversely, it can be very hard to 'let go' when we are under extreme emotional stress.

'Your shoes'

In 'your shoes', you endeavour to take on the position of another team player and experience the world through their eyes and ears. With practice, you will be able to develop similar feelings to those that the other person is experiencing, which will profoundly increase your ability to understand their point of view. (This should not be confused with having to agree with it, or with thinking 'they should. . .'.)

The most effective way to begin to develop stronger 'your shoes' position skills is to physically mirror your other team player's posture, gestures, breathing, language and so on.

'Fly on the wall'

The 'fly on the wall' takes the impartial observer's role: experiencing the situation as if you were outside of it. In the 'fly on the wall' position you are able to see yourself and everyone else at the same time, and to hear what is going on.

One way of checking that you are in a true 'fly on the wall' position is to notice whether you are still experiencing the emotions of yourself or the other persons. If you are, then you have not yet achieved the 'fly on the wall' position for that situation. This position is important to generate a sense of the whole, once again leading to greater understanding.

Use all three positions to increase your mental flexibility and ability to understand. Then return to 'my shoes' to make your decision and to decide if you can live with that decision.

Progress now

🔖 Choose a team player with whom you would like to get on better. Put two chairs facing each other and sit in one and imagine the team player is sitting in the other. Talking out loud, describe in detail how you experience him (or her) e.g. 'You talk rather loudly and always dress in black so that I feel . . .'

🔖 Now go and sit in the other chair and 'become' the other team player. Acting as if you were him (or her) and speaking out loud, describe in detail how he experiences you, e.g. 'You tend to sit bunched up and often don't meet my eyes . . .'

🔖 Now go to the other side of the room where you can, from a distance, see 'you' and 'the other team player' as if they were sitting in the chairs. Describe out loud and in detail what you notice about them: both similarities and differences, e.g. 'Their speaking volumes are very different. He talks about the future and I talk about the present. His body language is large and leaning forward whereas mine is . . .' Generate options for how 'you' could make changes to match his (or her) way of being in the world.

🔖 Walk back to 'you' and, as you do so, decide which options you will try out. Sit down and get back to really being you. Now imagine carrying out those behaviours that you have chosen. 'Videotape' future meet ups and notice what the outcome is. If the outcome is good – do it. If the outcome is unclear, ask yourself what else you need to reach a successful one (i.e. to build the relationship). Then go and do it.

CUTTING THROUGH THE FOG

Unfortunately, mind reading is generally not totally successful because we make sense of internal experiences through neurological, sociological and individual filters. It is therefore unlikely that we will guess accurately and precisely what someone else is experiencing, thinking or feeling. Instead of discovering their 'map of the world', their reality, we have a perception based on our own filters and end up with a 'me too' experience (i.e. we generalize, distort or delete the 'real' experience). This explains why so many people react with anger or incredulity if you say, 'I know where you are coming from' or 'I know how you are feeling'. They rightly know that you don't.

If you want to understand your team players' 'maps of the world', then you need to develop listening skills which are 'clean' of your filters and enable you to cut through theirs too. These listening skills require powerful questions that combat generalizations, deletions and distortions. But be very careful to maintain rapport or you may be accused of inquisition rather than friendly curiosity.

COMBATING GENERALIZATIONS

In order to communicate you will learn a word-symbol, like the word 'table' and then apply the symbol to other forms with a similar function. This ability to generalize promotes the rapid assimilation of diverse kinds of information but it can also generate confusion as to which table you mean or whether something is really a table at all. This is even more significant when we turn verbs into nouns such as 'I want support'. This assumes not only that we all want the same kind of 'support' but also that it exists (when in fact it is a process that happens through time).

Some common examples are:

1   **You hear:** All, every, no one, none, never, always. For example, 'My manager never listens to me.'
    Question: Reflect back the speaker's words — 'Never?', 'No one?', 'Always?' or ask, 'Was there ever a time when . . . ?'

2   **You hear:** Should/shouldn't, must/must not, have to. For example, 'I really should make that call.'
    Question: 'What would happen if you did/didn't . . . ?'

3   **You hear:** Can/can't, will/won't, may/may not, possible/impossible. For example, 'I can't say that to my boss.'
    Question: 'What stops you/him . . . ?'

COMBATING DELETIONS

We cannot not make sense of what we experience. In war, terrible atrocities occur that only make sense in that situation and to those involved in their perpetration – it was the best way they had at that time of making sense of their world even if it meant deleting information about other people's rights and the environment. Years on, revisiting such a place, it can often be as if it never happened – the best way that that community had of making sense of it is by deleting it. Even in the moment, humans have a rapid ability to delete parts of what someone is saying if it does not make sense to them. As you go out of the front door, try asking a teenager to wash up before watching television – what will you expect on return? This process of deletion has some profound implications in the area of human communication, as the following examples demonstrate.

1   **You hear:** 'What' is missing from the statement. For example, 'I am confused.'
    Question: 'About what specifically?', or 'how do you know?'

2   **You hear:** 'Who' or 'what' is missing from the statement. For example, 'They've got no idea.'
    Question: 'Who or what exactly . . . ?'

3   **You hear:** Implied comparison is missing – good, better, more, best, less, most, least. For example, 'She's a better person.'
    Question: 'Better than whom . . . ?'

4   **You hear:** The activity or movement is missing from the statement. For example, 'We have a problem with our communication.'
    (One way to test for this type of deletion is to put 'ongoing' in front of the word; for example, ongoing communication, ongoing relationship. If it makes sense, then you probably need to check it out.
    Question: 'Who is communicating/relating . . . to whom . . . about what?'

5   **You hear:** 'How' is missing from the statement. For example, 'She ignored me.'
    Question: 'How exactly . . . did she/he do that . . . could she/he do that?'

COMBATING DISTORTIONS

The figure on page 174 represents a 'visual paradox'. Because it presents conflicting information, the observer attempts to make sense of an apparently irrational figure. This *distortion* occurs because of the capacity of the brain to take in certain kinds of

information, in this case a two-dimensional set of lines, and transform it into something that is non-existent: a three-dimensional form on paper. You may hear someone say, 'Our business does not grow as long as we do not have a marketing budget.' This is a distortion in which two separate facts are joined together as if they made sense – even though there is no evidence of cause and effect – thereby creating a distortion in the mind. Consider the following examples:

1 **You hear:** A person mind reading when he/she presumes to know, without direct evidence, what another person is thinking or feeling. For example, 'I know what makes him tick.'
   Question: 'How do you know . . . ?'

2 **You hear:** That the owner of the statement has given the responsibility for their state and feelings to others. For example, 'This topic bores me' (i.e. makes me feel bored).
   Question: 'How does . . . cause . . . ?'

3 **You hear:** two statements that are linked in such a way that they are taken to mean the same thing. For example, 'He never speaks to me, he thinks I'm incompetent.'
   Question: 'How does . . . mean . . . ?'

4 **You hear:** A value judgement, where the person originally making the judgement is left out. For example, 'There is only one way to . . .'
   Question: 'According to whom?'

Progress now

When you hear any one of the cues on the left below, respond with the corresponding question on the right.

When you are comfortable with your team players, you can choose to use these powerful questions whenever you are curious about their view of the world. With this information you can then build improved relationships.

Cues			Responses
🔖 Never	—	🔖	Never?
🔖 Can't	—	🔖	What would happen if?

✎	Verb	— ✎	How, specifically?
✎	Noun	— ✎	What, specifically?
✎	Better	— ✎	Than what?

SUMMARY

✎ To be a team and to walk the brand, the players need to have a shared team understanding of the answers to the onion layers' questions 'what for', 'who', 'why', 'how', 'what', 'when' and 'where'.

✎ When conflict arises, change the onion level to check out what values/criteria/needs are not being met. Ask, 'What is important to you about that?', or 'If you had that, what would it do for you?' Then find (new) solutions that will meet those needs.

✎ Listening is more than knowing what you think. Step into the other person's shoes and experience the world through their eyes, ears and feelings. Then experience the situation as if you were a fly on the wall.

✎ Be curious to check out what the other person's 'map of the world' and 'reality' are like by using powerful questions to cut through the fog of generalizations, deletions and distortions.

CHAPTER 9

Your Best Experience

- Do you know how to become a world-class expert in exactly what you and your team need to learn?
- Do you know how to borrow from your own and others' experience?
- Do you know how to develop a best practice and install it in your team?

CREATING A PROCESS FROM EXPERIENCE

Experience is helpful in understanding processes that work across contexts. These experiences can both be borrowed/bought from others or taken from your own life. However, in order to be able to fully transfer your experience, you need to be able to structure it into a process or model.

Sometimes you will be able to identify the process or model yourself from just one experience and then be able to benefit from it many times, but usually you need to find a **pattern** that runs successfully. Sometimes you will run this pattern macro style, e.g. marrying a certain person, divorcing and then finding yourself in a similar relationship again; and sometimes you will run the pattern micro style: you catch yourself attracted to new colours of designer fabrics in a shop and become enthused at the idea of redecorating a room but do not feel compelled to take the next steps. In these situations, it is often helpful to have a facilitator or counsellor to help you to be 'objective' about the patterns you run and where you might change them. The same is true of a team that needs its coach. A coach should be able to notice patterns that a team is running and point them out, asking the players to 'run with' a pattern or process that works while suggesting they look at options for changing those that do not.

Disney Creativity Model

The Disney Creativity Process was modelled on Walt Disney and reflects the actual process he and his colleagues used to create those much-loved cartoon characters. It has five stages and if your team wants to innovate, then it could 'borrow' the process/model by following them.

1 Outline

Spend a few minutes describing the issue for which you wish to generate new ideas and move towards some future action. Ask one member of the team to act as notetaker and another to act as the timekeeper. Each of phases 2 through 5 normally takes between 5 and 20 minutes depending on the complexity of the issue and the time available.

2 Dreamer

Attention is directed to the longer term. This phase involves thinking in terms of the big picture to create new choices.

Typically, the head and eyes are up, the posture is symmetrical and relaxed. Breathing is from deep down in the stomach.

3 Realist

This phase is more action oriented, operating over a shorter timeframe than the Dreamer (say two weeks). This is a good time to consider procedures and operations – the 'how to' of the plan or the idea. It acts 'as if' the idea is possible. A storyboard can be produced as a powerful organizing and planning mechanism. Head and eyes are typically straight ahead or possibly slightly forward; the posture is symmetrical and slightly forward. Breathing is from slightly higher up in the chest.

4 Critic

This is the logical phase where what needs to be avoided, or what can go wrong, is identified. It is a search for potential sources of problems in both the short and the long term. It ensures that the key quality criteria are met. The typical posture is eyes down, head down and tilted to one side; the posture is asymmetrical, arms crossed and angular. Breathing may be more rapid and from high up in the chest.

5 Consolidation

The final phase is a return to a Realist phase in order to consolidate the four previous stages and to leave the process on a positive, forward-looking high note.

This process may be used in conjunction with brainstorming techniques, in which case *all* elements must be accumulated at the Dreamer stage, summarized and prioritized at the Realist stage and tested for overall feasibility at the Critic stage. The Consolidation stage takes the issue(s) forward and ensures that some action will result from the process.

BENCHMARKING

Benchmarking has become popular in organizations that want to 'get the basics right and then exceed expectations'. It is a helpful way of breaking patterns from the past or creating a new storyline. It is a way of creating experience in 'real time' rather than in waiting for experience that may put you behind the competition. It breaks the culture of 'not invented here' or 'not written in procedures' that prevails in 'blue' organizations (see Chapter 7 and Spiral Dynamics). Unfortunately, benchmarking that is inexpertly done can have dire consequences.

Here is a typical benchmarking process that does not even mention the main area of problem: the recipient. To make this work it must be installed sensitively to meet staff's needs too.

Benchmarking process

Select service – identify resources – identify partners – define and collect measures – compare performance – find best practice – plan change – implement and monitor

The benchmarking cycle

Plan

What is the scope of the study?

What problems exist?

What characteristics will you measure?

What information about the topic can you easily get?

What are the critical success factors?

Choose three teams to benchmark.

Do

Do the chosen three teams have a defined, documented process?

If not, how do they do it?

How is the process communicated to the 'process customers' and 'users'?

How are the users kept up to date on the process changes?

What is the management system of the process?

What aspects of the process are considered to be world class?

Check

Quantify your team's performance and check that there is a definite performance gap.

What does each of the partners you have benchmarked do about the process that is different from what you do?

What are the results?

Act

Select the process that seems to work the best, try it for a test period and evaluate the results.

A management team in the House of Commons, who were keen to ensure best practices in running the Palace of Westminster and other associated buildings, identified the 'best in class' in a number of processes that they thought they might like to adopt: dealing with enquiries and orders – in the holiday business; bar coding – to help with security of the treasures in

the buildings – as used in logistics; international couriers –
for handling post etc.

The managers then went out 'two by two' to interview a variety
of people involved in these processes: the managers, the staff
and the customers of the processes. Having seen the systems
working and knowing what went on, they were able, with the
support of senior managers and their peers, to convince
people internally to do something differently. Years on, these
practices are accepted as normal, everyday activities.

Progress now

- What would your team most like to excel in?
- Where in the world are teams that excel in this – in whatever field
  they operate in?
- Start working on a network to find a way of being able to find out how
  they do it: or just 'phone them direct (not much risk).
- Use the benchmarking process to identify how they do what they do.

INSTALLING EXPERIENCE

In order for the learning from benchmarking to 'take' in your team, you need to learn how to install a process so that it becomes integrated into the everyday life of your team. Failure to pay attention to the installation will mean that your team may become immune to new ideas, with comments such as, 'we tried something like that before' or 'just flavour of the month'.

Learn how your team learns

Before you start benchmarking other teams' processes, you first need to discover how your team learns. When you have discovered this process or model, then you will be able to install anything that the team wants to learn.

> The CEO of a charity said she felt better recently. She had felt like quitting because she had been brought in to change things but all she kept getting were negative responses to her suggestions, even lack of cooperation and a refusal to continue with flexibility. She wanted to collect management

information, to check the basis on which services were given and to seek best practices in staff utilization but they couldn't reach agreement on any of these issues because they didn't want to lose the special ethos of caring that they had.

And then the government issued new guidelines that meant that the charity could be closed down if these changes were not made. Suddenly it was 'as if a magic wand had been waved': the managers started to be nice to her and to agree to make changes, provided she told them what to do.

How this team learned had become evident. They valued the past. They moaned and hit out. They waited until things were as bad as they could be. They looked to an outside saviour to tell them what to do. They did it. They discovered new ways and felt better.

To learn how your team learns, think back to any change that has occurred to how the team operates or feels. Draw a storyboard of what happened (six pictures): the captions for the charity example might be:

1   Value past
2   Moan and fight
3   Worst news
4   Outside saviour
5   Plan how to
6   Feel good

Progress now

1   Discuss how you learn as a team activity.

   Alternatively, next time you have a team meeting, have one team player
   or a temporary member observe without taking part in the discussions.
   Your team will run the same pattern for learning and moving forward
   over and over again.

2   Record how you learn on a storyboard to help you focus on the process.
   Use it to install new experiences from elsewhere or as benchmarked
   from other teams (or to have more choices in how you learn as a team).

SUMMARY

- Experience is useful if it gives you a process to use across contexts.

- You can most easily value experience if you transfer learning from somewhere else in your life.

- If you benchmark experience from other teams, look for a process that is repeatable.

- Work out how your team learns and use your learning process or model to install experience from elsewhere.

CHAPTER 10

Balancing Your Best Team with the Rest of Your Life

- ℚ Do you want to succeed with your best team, balance your life and experience personal delight?

- ℚ Do you want to reduce unhealthy experiences and increase healthy ones?

- ℚ Do you want your 'inner team' to be there for you?

YOU AS A TEAM

There is only one you, but it may sometimes seem as if there are different parts – the worker you, the sporty you, the parent you, the adventuring you, the little child you and so on. If you think back to times when you have found it hard to make a decision or have made one at deep personal cost, then you have probably felt that your inner team was being split or that one of your parts was being ignored.

It is when your inner team becomes fragmented that problems can start for you. Just as an outer team can become fragmented and dysfunctional, so can an inner team. If you continue to ignore any part of you, it may start to 'play up'. Some people refer to these as 'wake-up calls'. These may be in the form of 'unexpected' accidents, illnesses or personal upheavals such as job loss and divorce. These are games that you can play on yourself that you will also practise in your outside teams. These games can be ones that you have played both inside and outside for so long that it can be very hard for you to recognize that you are using them to have power over another team player. Eric Berne has probably done more than anyone to list 'the games people play'.

THE DRAMA TRIANGLE

One of the ways that you can explain people's behaviour is by understanding how the 'drama triangle' operates. In essence, this is where part of you may sabotage yourself by taking on a specific role in the outside world. When you are unclear of what you want or how to achieve it, you can easily fall into what is often referred to as 'the blame culture'. **You** have a problem but it is preferable to offload it, so you take up any of the three roles in the triangle:

🐾 **Victim: poor me!** I do not like the situation. If only it were not for my 'wooden leg', I could achieve great things. Someone should take care of me and help me achieve something better. If they don't, I'll start to kick up a fuss so that they have to take notice and help me. They had better hurry up and change their behaviour.

🐾 **Persecutor: it's their fault!** I do not like the situation. Somebody has let me down, how dare they! I shall put my energy and my anger into finding someone on whom I can vent my anger. When I find them, they had better get ready to change their behaviour.

🐾 **Rescuer: they cannot cope without me!** I do not like the situation. It isn't fair. The victim isn't strong enough to sort it out

and the persecutor is being really mean. I'd better have a word
with them, so that they can change their behaviour.

Each of the three roles looks to what the protagonist does not
want and how someone else should change their behaviour. This
is a game of power that denies responsibility. The drama triangle
is a powerful force with inevitability about it ('here we go
again'). We can switch roles but often have a preferred one (note
the rescuer is often perceived, by the persecutor, as a persecutor
who is victimizing the original persecutor).

How to stay off the drama triangle

🔊 **Decide what you want.** The key to new behaviour is having a clear
idea of the outcome that you want, a set of helpful beliefs and an
identity of team player. A compelling goal that is lived is so
powerful that it is attractive to you and to others. Check it is a
rich picture and that you know which bit is up to you.

🔊 **Check the knock-on effect.** If you have a vision which compels
you to take action, you can expect a reaction. So before taking
action, ask yourself: 'If I had this outcome (a) what would it do for
me – and do I want that? (b) What effect will it have on others?
Step into their shoes to experience the outcome from their point of
view. (See Chapter 8 for how to do 'your shoes'.)

Ⓞ **Generate alternative solutions and 'just do it'.** 'If you always do what you always did, you will always get what you always got.' This means taking the lead in trying something new.

Ⓞ **If someone comes to you for help, give them seeds and a plough, not a loaf.** It is very common to hear people describe their ideal team culture as 'empowering'. Games are disempowering: clearly so in persecutor and victim but often challengingly so in rescuer. Rescuer feeds on beliefs such as, 'I should take responsibility as a manager' or 'I should stand up for others'. Unfortunately, all of these beliefs in certain contexts can be disempowering.

A team leader was struggling to manage a team member. Each time the team member failed to perform well, he put off giving her this feedback and, instead, stepped in to pick up the pieces. At last, the team leader's director said that this was unacceptable: the subordinate must be given clear feedback, clear goals and either take appropriate action or be dismissed.

The team leader asked the director if she could say these things to the team member on his behalf. The team leader was terrified of the emotional outbursts of the team member: they were unpredictable and could range from fury to tears (thereby hooking either inaction through rescuer or victim from the team leader). The director was tempted to say yes (and be hooked into rescuer) – she knew how well she would sort out that team member. Alternatively, she was tempted to say she would sit in during the meeting just in case things went awry. Both would be actions based on the presupposition that the team leader could not manage (victim) – in which case, what was he doing in the job? Instead, the director spent two hours role-playing the possible scenarios with the team leader who, eventually, went into the performance review meeting with a new-found confidence.

The first meeting was one of 'damage limitation' only, i.e. feedback given, goals set, actions agreed. Now the team leader/team member relationship has developed into a new trust and the team member has started to seek suggestions from the team leader to help her improve her performance.

Although tempted to play rescuer, the director used an empowering strategy that allowed each of the three people to do their own jobs and to do them properly.

Progress now

🔖 Notice, when you have a dilemma or problem, how often, under this stress, you enter the blame culture and take on a role of persecutor, victim or rescuer. This has a feeling of 'here we go again'. Resolve to stay off the drama triangle in any transaction by having direct dealings with the other person, with no third party, and taking responsibility for having a compelling goal that takes account of the needs of all stakeholders or team players (both internal and external).

🔖 When someone comes to you for help, take on board the presupposition that they already have all the resources they need to achieve their outcomes and use your skills to facilitate their self-belief to take positive action themselves.

SICK TEAMS

Wilfred Bion's work on team dynamics also gives us insight into what happens in teams when people fail to take responsibility for themselves as team leaders or team players – and what happens to them. Just as individuals can become ingrained in playing games and become sick, so can whole teams.

Bion describes several types of unhealthy team:

Fight or flight

In some teams, when things go wrong there is no structure in place for team players to have their say – they feel disempowered. They start to grumble and to become dysfunctional, waiting for a leader to emerge. When a leader does take the reins, team players will then either become angry and resist change – fighting the team and the very leader that they wanted – or hide away pretending that change is not happening and then leave, thereby fleeing from the team and the leader.

In some organizations, a new director or team leader will be appointed, but be found wanting within a few months. The cycle may be repeated several times until a restructure is called for or the team disbanded. This can happen as an inner team, where you allow one thing after another to dominate your life (your job, a new relationship, a new hobby) but, as soon as you achieve what you wanted, you decide you want something different.

Messianic hope

Some teams can fall into despondency when the outside situation (e.g. the economic climate, the market, the technology) changes radically. Team players can feel overwhelmed by the new situation and not believe that they have the internal resources to once more be in control of their own destiny. Instead they give way to hopes for salvation from some superior being who 'knows the way'. When a messiah appoints themself then there will be initial relief while team players filter for evidence of a track record, an inspirational message and a new way of behaving (the honeymoon period). But when the messiah fails to deliver or breaks a taboo, then the team calls for them to be publicly renounced.

In consequence, leaders who turn situations around are rarely kept in power: the ordinary team players need to reassert themselves. The warning to our inner team is that no one part of us can be sufficient in the long term – all our parts need to be in play if there is to be inner harmony.

Projection and scapegoat

There is good and bad in every team and in every person. However, it is not always comfortable to acknowledge imperfections in yourself – often it is easier to blame someone else. This is called projecting from yourself onto another. For example, in an organization, the purchasing department can be blamed for slowing things down when, in reality, it is your poor specification that does not allow them to do their job efficiently.

An individual can scapegoat part of themselves: 'If it were not for my (angina, sick mother, mortgage, etc.), then I would do what I want.' Suggested solutions will be rebutted with the game 'yes, but . . .'. The scapegoat is the cloak for not taking responsibility and challenging action.

The management team of a manufacturing company had had their heads down working hard for so long that they could hardly bare to be away from their desks for more than an hour. Yet the figures were quite clear: year after year, the market was slipping away from them. The managing director slumped in his chair and related to the team facilitator his problems at home; the finance director explained his fears that he was forgetting significant but small details, the sales and marketing director was off sick with a 'bad foot that had gone gangrenous'. Similar tales of woe were forthcoming from other team members. This was a team that was not just sick in parts but riddled with it.

And yet the team was enormously fond of each other, clinging together amongst the wreckage. They were the 'stickers' who, years ago had chosen to stay when others, seeing the going getting tough, had gone in flight. And they had fought every inch of the way to save their jobs and those who worked for them. They had taken on worldwide contracts that paid little margin, they had taken on other work that added little value and demeaned their skills, and they had stopped investment. They had fought on until they had been bought out.

Now the fight had turned inwards: they knew they could not continue as they had but neither could they leave. This inward fight was resulting in parts of them becoming sick, and no one was immune. The sickness was in the team system or ingrained behaviour patterns and it became inevitable that depression, anxiety and illness would increase. The parent company that had acquired them took decisive action and broke up the team.

INTEGRATING YOUR CONFLICTING PARTS

The aim of the following steps is to integrate your beliefs or parts so that they complement each other, stop fighting: giving you more choice and resources. This exercise requires the help of a partner.

1   Identify the conflicting beliefs or parts that your partner has and notice the physiology associated with each. If there are several, ask your partner to identify and label the main two.

2   Ask your partner to put the conflicting parts in different hands. For example, you can say, 'Put the part of you that believes X in your left hand.' Choose the hand that your partner uses when describing that belief. Ask, 'What pictures, sounds and feelings do you have associated with that part of you (in your left hand)?' If any of these senses are forgotten, ask your partner to describe them further. Put the other part in the other hand and go through the same process.

3   Ask each part to experience the other and describe what it sees, feels and hears. At this stage the different parts will typically dislike each other hence some of the reason for the conflict. Notice any changes in physiology as your partner considers the different parts.

4   Find the positive intention and purpose of each part. Make sure that each part does recognize and accept the positive intention of the other. Ask such questions as, 'The part of you that likes to be

201

spontaneous, what does that do for you?' When you get the answer, ask your partner to 'say thank you to the part that gives you that'.

5   Identify the goal that they share – ask such questions as, 'If you had both love and achievement (identified as the positive intentions in 4), what would those both do for you? What would that be like?' The conflict is directly interfering with the achievement of their overall purposes.

6   Have each part describe the resources held by the other part that it needs to accomplish its goals. Get an agreement from the parts to combine their resources – this is an exchange of gifts. If the parts cannot accept the resources or gifts that the other part has, ask, 'What else does that part need to be able to accept it?'

7   Have the parts move together at the same time so that a new integrated whole is being created. Often you will notice that your partner automatically brings their hands together when doing this; if not, you may say, 'Bring your two parts together until your hands are clasped.' Check the physiology to ensure that it incorporates the physiology of the two parts and that the hands stay together. If not, revisit 6 above.

8   Test the validity of this new identity by having your partner consider future contexts in which their behaviour will be different with these parts integrated. For example, 'So what will you do then?'

PARTS PARTY

In Buddhism, there are three key concepts: the Buddha (the idea of a perfect role model), the Dharma (your journey or path to follow) and the Sangha (your community of supporters). It is important to build up a team of outer friends and supporters who encourage you towards your dreams; equally important, is the team of inner friends to support you. If you allow voices and pictures of people close to you to aggressively dominate your inner world, then you will feel disturbed. Many people can conjure up inner voices and pictures of people whom they can sense to be close to them and have their support both in daydreams and in sleep.

Progress now

Practise pushing away internal representations of unsupportive people and quietening/changing the tone of any antagonistic voices. Step into 'fly on the wall' (see Chapter 8) and see both them and yourself. When they and you are distant 'from yourself', find out what these energy-sinking parts of you need in order to collaborate with your inner supporters so that you can celebrate more of your life.

SUMMARY

- Take care of your inner team in order to find balance in your life.

- Pay attention to all of your 'parts': they all have a contribution to your well-being and your developing your potential.

- Beware of playing mind games that can escalate into ever-increasing stress for you and others. Instead, take responsibility for your experience and learn from it: that way you can make a difference in the world.

- By concentrating on inner harmony and integrating your various parts, your inner team or Sangha will be there to support you, whatever you face.

CHAPTER 11

Going Beyond Your Comfort Zone

- Do you want to be continually learning and developing?
- Do you wonder what the future holds for teams?
- Do you want to manage that change?

LONGER-TERM DEVELOPMENT

In Chapter 3, you were encouraged to create a well-formed outcome of your dream team. Now it is time to put this into the wider context of your entire life to see if there is more that you would add.

> # Progress now
>
> ◊ Start by drawing a picture of how you experience your life now. When you have finished, date it. If possible, talk it through with a friend (a supporter, part of your supporters or Sangha – see Chapter 10).
>
> ◊ If you are enjoying the drawing, skip to the last Progress Now in this chapter, otherwise continue through the others in sequence.

Often, people are unclear about who they are and what they value or believe in. Your outside life is feedback of how your inner team (that is, you) is working, and so it is worth thinking through your roles and core values to see whether these are a true reflection of who you want to be.

Teaching can be a tough profession and some teachers long for 'a normal job'. After having taught for many years, one such teacher applied for and was offered a job in a large IT corporation training customers in software applications.

The job was certainly a challenge. Learning the software, inspiring the customers and working in an entirely different culture – as well as coping with family demands – filled each day. But, increasingly, there was a niggle. Learning and teaching so much technical information was not really her – she needed to make a difference to people at a deeper level. She wanted to help people believe that they could do whatever they wanted, just as she had shown she could. So she enrolled on a neurolinguistic programming practitioner course, ran courses in personal development at the local further education college, and then decided to return to teaching at a secondary school as Head of ICT, while continuing to develop her counselling skills.

All of these fitted with her inner mission to make a deep difference to people. This enabled her to cope with the tired surroundings of the school, the inadequacy of the ICT resources and even the low ratio of staff to students.

YOUR PURPOSE IN LIFE

Just as an external team needs to know its purpose, so do you. Sometimes, people seem to be born with a 'mission' or 'calling', but most often this is something that unfolds within them as they learn about themselves in relation to the world, experiences or other people.

If you are unaware of your purpose in life, you are in danger of aligning yourself to someone who is clear on theirs and who can inspire you, whether or not it is right for you. Organisations are full of people who 'ended up there by chance' or who 'were only looking for a six month filler' and who stayed an unfulfilled lifetime. Finding your purpose in life is therefore a task of exploration using both your internal resources and tapping into those of your supporters or Sangha (see Chapter 10) in order for you to have a good sense of what is right for you.

Progress now

Imagine that you are a number of years in the future, celebrating your birthday. At your party are all the people whom you really want to be there: your friends past and present, your colleagues whom you respect and like, your family whom you are close to and people whom you enjoy meeting in the community.

Silence is called and, one by one, a representative of each of the four groups of guests starts to talk about you in celebration of what you mean to them. Focus in turn on who those four people would be and think through what you would most like to hear them saying about you.

Write down what you have heard these people saying about you. Think through what this means about who you are and what your life means to others.

WHAT MAKES YOU SPECIAL?

As you start to think about your purpose in life, you will begin to realize that your uniqueness identifies who you are and that this can be refreshing or challenging for others: your being with someone can make a difference to their thoughts and feelings; your focus and wishes will bring direction to a team. One of the assumptions in this book is that 'you cannot not communicate'. Others may not communicate with you in the way you would like, but just by being you do communicate.

Sometimes the message that you communicate is confused. If you do not 'walk your talk' then people will usually go by your non-verbal behaviour (someone shaking their head while saying that they agree may not be believed). Make sure that you receive feedback on how you are coming across to others – a conflict between how you wish to come across and how you do may well denote that your 'inner team' is not balanced.

Progress now

What makes you special? (a task in pairs)

Discovering who you are

1   List five emotions that you are sure to experience during any one week.

2   Take each emotion in turn and identify a specific instance during the past week when you felt that emotion strongly. Then have your partner ask you the following questions:

   a)   In that situation, what were you [emotional] about?

   b)   What is significant about [answer to a]?

   c)   Why (or how) does [answer to b] matter?

   Your partner repeats question c (that is, 'Why does [answer to previous c] matter?') until you get to the 'end of the line'. If the answer is in the 'negative', your partner asks, 'What would be the opposite of that?'

   Repeat this series of questions for each of the other emotions.

Finding your identity

3   Look at the five sets of answers to question 2 and identify the patterns that underlie them all by considering: 'What am I always caring about?' and 'What am I always trying to do regarding what I care about?'

4   These are fundamental elements of your identity and what makes you special. It may be useful to enrich the powerful expression of some words or phrases in these identity elements by asking, 'What does that mean?' and/or 'How do I go about doing that?'

Using your identity statements to be special

5   a)   Identify something you want to be motivated to do but are not. Consider: 'In what ways is it an opportunity to fulfil my identity?' Then consider: 'In what ways would not doing it be a violation of who I am?'

    b)   Identify something you have been trying to decide about. Evaluate which alternative best fulfils 'who I am'.

THE FUTURE OF TEAMS: FORCED, SHORT-LIVED, CULTURALLY DIVERSE, GLOBAL, VIRTUAL

Forced, short-lived teams

Most of us will experience many teams, over our lifetime, not only in our different roles but also as new members join and leave a team we are already part of. Often teams are short-lived or project-based, requiring everyone to be exceptionally skilled in order to speed through the phases that teams must go through in order to perform effectively. As organizations merge, implementation teams compete to collapse timescales even further, and as people are required to become more multitasked, there will be more demands on people to perform in teams where they may no longer have specialist knowledge but where teamworking needs to produce creative solutions to challenges. Nina Minchin describes the challenge that she faced at her school and how she dealt with it (see Interview).

NINA MINCHIN

Now Head of Information and Communications Technology at Trinity School, Newbury – this took place at a previous school

DIVERSE SPECIALISTS FORCED TO BE A TEAM

Drugs and sex education at school

It looked like it was going to be a special year. I had been asked to head a team of teachers from varied subject areas to deliver personal and social education to 15/16-year-olds. My team was made up of scientists, musicians, historians, mathematicians and me. How was I to sell to this varied group of people the delights of delivering topics such as drugs and sex education?

Our meetings started off being a bit of a battleground: such comments as, 'I came into education to teach maths not sex' and 'If you think I'm going to swot up on drugs, you've got another think coming'. I assured them that I would not put them into a situation where they were compromised, and that they had to trust me. All I would ask was that they would not close their minds and that they support me in the sessions. I wanted their ideas. I wanted them to own the sessions. But *I* would make them happen.

I wanted to set up sessions on disability and alcohol abuse, amongst others. I visited a day centre for people with disabilities and invited six people from varying backgrounds to come to the school and spend time with each tutor group. I also asked them to supply wheelchairs for the students to 'try out' in the corridors because I wanted them to experience what it was like to be in a wheelchair and the issues around that, such as invasion of personal space.

My wary teacher team was relieved to know that they were not going to be stuck with twenty-five 16-year-olds on their own, having to talk about the issues around disability – and started to show some interest. That was fine by me, provided they were present. I was convinced that my new 'friends' with disabilities would captivate the children, and I was right. Bearing in mind that the yeargroup consisted of 250 teenagers, the corridors were fairly active for part of the session: with students careering around in wheelchairs. Others did spend time asking questions and generally 'finding out what it was about being disabled', and yet others listened to a general talk from the day centre manager. One of my new, 'friends' was an ex-biker whom I put with some particularly difficult lads. It worked: they were intrigued and affected by him, and he with them.

This sort of event had never happened before in the school and I hadn't realized that my fame had spread to the hierarchy. Yet, on the morning of the visit, the deputy heads came and offered to make tea for our visitors and promised their support. After the event, members of my team, and others, came in person or wrote to me, thanking me for involving them and saying what a valuable experience it had been for them – never mind the students. Meanwhile, my team seemed to have grown.

My second challenge with my team was to do a session around alcohol abuse. Again, my team was nervous in their responses but, by now, there was some feeling that Nina would not dump them with worksheets; more confidence and interest pervaded our meetings. I told them that I had spoken to Alcoholics Anonymous and that two people were prepared to come and talk to the children en masse. Some negativity was around: 'Well I can't see the likes of . . . sitting still for an hour listening to someone talking about that!' But they soon eased up when I told them that they themselves just had to sit in the hall for this session.

The two people who came were captivating. The man started his talk by saying, 'I remember the first time I hit my wife'. From then on, he related a catalogue of destructive behaviour. You could have heard a pin drop. Other staff sidled in as the word spread that this man had a worthwhile tale to tell. The kids were wonderful, and so were my team. Again I had notes from some of them thanking me for involving them . . . and perhaps even more pleasing were the notes from the children. They also wrote notes to their guests, a man and a woman who had told their stories with such honesty.

I started by saying that it was a special year. It was because I started off by wondering how I could make a difference and, by the end, I knew I had: to my team, to the hierarchy, to many of the other staff and, most importantly, I knew I had reached some children who would not be reached by any other means but by the raw honesty of actual experience: that wider 'team' I had reached in a small way.

Without these team building skills, short-lived teams may become a constant source of frustration for those who can imagine how good it could be – even if you are supposed to be enjoying yourself. Frances Cooper's story shows how short-lived teams still need to be set up correctly.

FRANCES COOPER

Master yachtsman and Q.Learning consultant

SHORT-LIVED TEAMS

Sailing on the Solent

Starting in October up until the 8 December, the winter series begins in the sailing world. Every Sunday, there is a mad panic around 8 a.m. when the crews arrive and get the boats ready, have bacon sandwiches, cups of coffee, sort their clothes out, check out the tides, find out weather patterns, carry out safety briefings, allocate roles and catch up on the other people and what has happened to them in the past week (or year) since they last met. The race starts around 9.30 a.m. and generally lasts four hours, by which time you are ready for a drink in the bar while you find out the results.

The celebration at the end is something we are good at on *Amandla Kulu* – the other bits have room for improvement! With so little time and so much to do in the first hour, not everything gets done. Prioritization means that about the top two or three things are done and the rest fall by the wayside. As a result, as a team we 'storm'· and 'form'. Rarely do we get to the 'norm' and even more rare is evidence of 'performing'.

Culturally diverse teams

Team complexity nowadays often includes people operating out of their comfort zones of 'expert', with much collapsed timespans for achievement of goals, and with the increased likelihood of a mix of cultures, nationalities and needs. It is essential for such teams to pay even closer attention to people's motivation 'buttons' and to take on other team players' points of view by 'stepping' even more exquisitely into their 'shoes' (Chapter 8).

Cultural diversity is usually an issue for those without power, not for those with it. It can be a difficult task to get those within an organization or institution to perceive prejudice or racism. This is especially true in organizations that acquire others, but it can also be a blindspot for even the best intentioned, as Jonathan Harris describes in his interview.

JONATHAN HARRIS

MD of Learning Matters, an educational publishing company

VALUING RACIAL AND CULTURAL DIVERSITY

At church

When we lived in Tooting, we went to a very multicultural church where I was churchwarden for a while. My experience there was around power, blindness to racism, and blindness to the variety of other cultures. All the office holders were white, but many of the members were black and Asian. The whites believed that if any of the ethnic minorities wanted to hold an office of authority they simply had to stand for election and they would be elected. The actual experience of the blacks and Asians was that they had stood for office and had not been elected and therefore had given up trying. So the whites believed they were part of an inclusive, multicultural community, while the minorities believed that they were held back by white-dominated authority. There was an assumption of power on the part of the whites, an assumption of powerlessness on the part of the blacks and Asians, a blindness to racism on the part of the whites who believed they were part of a healthy Christian group, and a blindness to the variety of other cultures in the white belief that blacks and Asians were part of the same community. Meanwhile, the blacks thought the Asians were trying to be part of the white power bloc, and the Asians thought the blacks didn't do enough to help themselves.

Breaking down the barriers that these, largely unconscious, positions created was hard going. We created an infrastructure of house groups in which some were led and hosted by black people, and to which some of the powerful white people went. This helped, but the most difficult issue was dealing with whether the fact that if racial minorities believed the church was racist meant that it was, or whether this was a prejudice on the part of the minorities. There was a wide range of white approaches to this that made for lively discussions. Fortunately, the outcome was an acceptance, at institutional level at least, that the perception of racism equated to racism, and support for minority candidates for positions of power.

In spite of the difficulty of short-lived and culturally diverse teams, the same good practices in team development apply if you want to succeed. Clear purpose, shared values and rapport, flexible behaviours and some common ground rules, as well as an appreciation of each other's environments, continue to be vital to success. Claire Jones describes in her interview how a successful team developed, with a little effort, out of what was initially a dysfunctional culturally diverse team.

CLAIRE JONES

Business Development Director, Oracle Corporation – an experience in a previous company

SHORT-LIVED AND CULTURALLY DIVERSE TEAM

A large-scale bid

Features of the team:

1   Formed with staff from three separate companies, each of which offered distinct skills.

2   Two British companies and one American, with administrative staff from temp. agencies.

3   The size of the team started at about a dozen for the first phase, and peaked at over 50 during the second phase.

4   The purpose of the team was to win a large RAF contract.

We took a while to bond because:

1   The initial team was based on premises belonging to one of the British companies, and so there was a big 'visitor' dynamic.

2 There was little appreciation of or respect for the skills and experience of the companies for each other and, by extension, the individual staff members.

3 There were quite strong cultural differences, including preferred working times, the way we addressed each other, and acceptable socializing activities. And that was just the British. Add in the Americans and you had a whole new ball game.

Things that helped us bond during phase 1 (3 months):

1 We had a clear common purpose as a team.

2 As individuals, we all had a reason for wanting to get through to the next phase (not necessarily the same, e.g. the Americans wanted to stay in the UK as much as develop their careers).

3 We all put in a lot of hours – this does not necessarily denote quality of output, but it was taken as a signal of individual commitment, which earned respect.

Bonding really took off for phase 2 (6 months) because:

1 We'd shared a win in being shortlisted for the next phase

2 The core members of the team shared a high level of respect

for their colleagues, which communicated itself to new members.

3   We moved to new premises in a neutral building.

4   We travelled on business together, which gave us social time together outside working hours.

5   We started organizing social activities we could all buy into, for team members and their partners.

6   We developed our own culture about what we valued as good behaviour and what was not useful.

7   We had a dress-down Friday.

Global teams

As international business teams become more common, people will inevitably gain greater knowledge about global issues and there will be an expectation of shared knowledge and resources to achieve ever larger goals. In the UK, the drive by government over the last few years has been to measure standards of public services, to set targets and to achieve consistency of quality. Perhaps nowhere has this been more successfully achieved than in the area of the English Blood Service that is renowned for quality worldwide. This special competence is leading individuals to contribute on a world stage to help develop blood services around the world, as Patrick Sullivan describes in his interview.

PATRICK SULLIVAN

Patrick Sullivan is Head of Operations, Diagnostic Services, Development and Research, National Blood Service, England

GLOBAL TEAMS

A matter of life and death

Eighty per cent of the blood collected is used by only 20% of the world's population (predominantly the richest countries): is this a problem? Yes, it is. Apart from the impact of globalization, it cannot be right that such a fundamentally important and altruistic act, which gives life to so many, results in such a disparity in standards of safety. Nor is it right that so many who need a transfusion are denied one due to the lack of access.

What can be done? First, organizations with leverage and influence need to work together as towards a clear outcome that might be 'to align blood safety in all countries for the benefit of humanity'. The reality makes this all but impossible to achieve. Nonetheless, striving for this outcome will make the life or death difference for many.

Personal networks will, of course, continue to be important. The possibility of a 'virtual team', comprising committed individuals, is emerging – drawn from such organizations as the World Health Organization (WHO), the Pan American Health Organization (PAHO) and the International Society of Blood Transfusion (ISBT) and the more advanced national blood services that have indicated a willingness to make expert people available. Working together, this virtual and diverse team can help developing blood services to improve more quickly and overcome in some way barriers that include: political and governmental structures, cultural and religious differences, lack of funding, and language barriers.

These constraints must not be a barrier to progress. We must work with the natural leaders in developing blood services, whose presence is vital to their organizations' gaining momentum and making real and significant change.

In a few years' time, we will be able to look back to the present day and say, 'Yes, we made a difference. We helped more people in more countries to close this unique circle: that in which the community gives blood so that the community may receive life.'

Virtual teams

A future for teams – beyond forced membership, people's comfort zones, collapsed timescales, cultural, racial and national diversity, and global responsibility that are already upon you, and that will become an increasing feature of teams as e-working gets under way – is that of the virtual team. A virtual team is one that may bring together many (semi) autonomous or independent people or organizations under a shared purpose yet who may rarely or never meet. For these teams to succeed, sensitivity to needs and flexibility become paramount.

Some organizations wish to foster the added value that multidisciplinary teams bring, to such an extent that they invest in the training and facilitation of a network of teams. Adam Baker describes in his interview how, at AIT, the T-Groups were seen as the backbone that helped the company in its rapid growth from 1986 to 2002 and helped it to come fifth in the *Sunday Times* 'Best Company to Work For' list and winner of 'Most Fun Company to Work For'.

ADAM BAKER

Strategic Director, AIT (an E-CRM company)

DEVELOPING A MULTIDISCIPLINARY CULTURE

The T-Group system at AIT was designed to bring people closer together and foster an environment of open communication between all levels of the company. T-Groups consist of multidisciplined groups of up to nine people. Each group has a leader whose role is to facilitate discussion within the group. T-Groups enable:

- The staff to ask questions of the management and vice versa

- A communications structure to deliver face to face information and receive quality feedback

- 'Taking the pulse': a mechanism to get views and issues from all parts of the company

- Pastoral care: each individual has someone independent of their career manager and task manager to turn to for advice and support

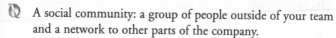

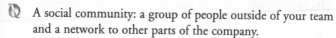   A social community: a group of people outside of your team and a network to other parts of the company.

In the UK, these groups meet face-to-face in their groups. In the USA, due to an acquisition, the offices and workers are geographically spread, so these meetings are 'virtual' via conference call. The two principal challenges that faced the groups were, how to build these mini relationships and how to bring together people from the acquired and acquiring companies. Each group was chosen to have equal representation from each office or remote location. Many of the staff of the acquired company had not met each other or people from the acquired company.

Issues started being raised by these groups, which went some way to uniting them as they felt they had a common cause, but there were many comments from the group leaders that meetings were more like business meetings and had no social content or bonding.

The Group leaders devised different ways of getting the meetings to become more social, these include:

   Social time: devoting 15 minutes of each meeting for each person to tell the group something about themselves or what they have done outside of work, favourite food, film etc.

🔌 Book recommendations: suggest a book for the group to read and discuss for the next meeting

🔌 Group twinning: in a similar way to the town twinning system, groups from the UK and the USA would twin. This would involve sharing a conference call once a quarter to speak to each other, but would also be used to create one-to-one relationships between members of the groups, e.g. when someone visited the UK they would know someone and have a point of contact. Each group would interpret the twinning differently, from sending photos of the view from their desk, to information on the projects they were working on

Over three months, the groups really started to come together and rapport was built between the people in the acquired and acquiring company, as well as between people in the acquired company. The model proved so successful that it was piloted in the UK where small numbers of staff were constantly out on a client's site and so unable to make the traditional face-to-face UK meetings.

Progress now

Here are some helpful hints from Julia Figg, Projects Director, Intrum, on how to cope in diverse teams:

- Learn to be flexible in your approach, even using different styles within the same meeting.

- As the leader of the team, don't try to force the others to adopt your 'cultural' style but respect the cultural differences and use them well.

- Learn to be able to 'make fun' out of your own culture and use this as a tool for building rapport within the team.

- Organise team-building events and base them in different countries in which your team members are based.

- Never assume familiarity. Always address a person by their title until invited to do otherwise.

- Be aware that it is normal in some cultures to conduct the real business of a meeting over lunch or coffee, when the atmosphere is somewhat more relaxed.

- Do not assume that non-native English speakers will be fluent in English. Check every now and then for comprehension, being sensitive to the fact that some people will not like to admit that they have not understood what you have been saying.

Meanwhile, in looking at the requirements that the government puts on the public services to provide a 'seamless service' to the client, virtual teams, bringing together professionals from several government agencies, may need to blur the edges of professional knowledge and move along a continuum of team organization. In *A Multidisciplinary Approach to Rehabilitation* (Butterworth-Heinemann 2000), Kumar has listed the teams on this continuum as including:

- *Functional teams.* Describes a situation where a number of different professionals are consulted independently of each other to provide a service directly to the service user. The organizing principle is the discipline.

- *Multidisciplinary teams.* The organizing principle is still functional, i.e. the individual departments still recruit, manage and allocate the resources. The functional departments then allocate staff to a particular area of work.

- *Interdisciplinary teams.* This is a further move to organizing staff and resources around a particular group of service users.

- *Transdisciplinary teams.* The furthest point along the continuum. The focus in this type of team is more on providing a consistent approach to care and less on who provides the care. Many professions may be employed as part of these teams; however, roles are not strictly defined in professional terms. Cross-training and multiskilling are emphasized over and above profession-specific training, although each profession contributes unique approaches and techniques when that is appropriate. The aim of this type of team is to reduce duplication, particularly of assessment, and to ensure that service users receive consistent information and treatment, with the user needs at the centre of the interventions.

Everything that has been said about teams applies with a vengeance once the form of communication relies on email, occasional long distance phone calls, and possibly, video conferencing. Team building without meetings requires great communication skills, which includes a willingness to work in the other team players' preferred ways – even if it runs against your own style.

Finally, Julia Figg of Intrum offers some advice regarding home-based workers who are part of a virtual team.

JULIA FIGG

Project Director, Intrum Justicia
(Credit Management Solutions)

VIRTUAL TEAM MEMBERS STILL HAVE A NEED TO BELONG

Home-based staff

With regard to virtual teams, it is worth bearing in mind that some people – even highly motivated people – really do need to feel part of a team and can become isolated/demotivated if working alone for long periods, especially home-workers. In those cases, my advice is to encourage the team leader to make contact on a regular basis (not too frequent as to become intrusive/to give a feeling of being checked on but enough to ensure that the individual does not feel neglected). Plenty of dialogue between the team members is also to be encouraged. Email is not the best tool for this purpose (too impersonal); video conferencing can be a help with an established team but *never* use it as a replacement for face-to-face meetings. The importance of the 'informal' aspects of face-to-face meetings is also not to be underestimated. It's so important and yet companies often try to cut costs of travel – in my view, this is a false economy.

PROCESS FOR MANAGING CHANGE

Here are a few actions for managing change based on ideas from *Spiral Dynamics* by Chris Cowan and Don Beck:

🕦 Change *from* what, *to* what? When you have a team that functions well enough you will want to make sure that you are very clear on this and that you talk it and walk it in such a way that it is powerfully compelling for you and for everyone with whom you come in contact. Any uncertainty will be amplified in your organization.

🕦 Estimate the potential for change. You need to be sensitive to the states that your team is in, i.e. are the team players open to change (with potential for more complex functioning), arrested (caught by barriers in themselves or their situation) or closed (blocked by feeling threatened or by lack of personal resources).

🕦 Create solutions for problems. If you raise the threat of 'enemies at the gates' with the expectation that more complex thinking will emerge, do not be surprised if the walls go up instead and the person or group retreats into a psychological fortress of denial. If stability is the key issue, bring order. If fear is draining productivity, deliver the bad news quickly and then make things safe. This will allow excess energy to resurge and to be available for exploring the next, more complex issue.

🖎 Change does not occur unless the boat rocks. Make sure that your people understand your environment as well as you do. If you are a team in a company, you will probably know your share price, the bank lending rates, sterling's value, and the likely impact of joining the euro – why? If you are in a public body, then you will read about the prime minister's speeches, study how your leader of the council or minister thinks, and keep an eye on best value, modernization ideas and CPA's – why? Because, knowing shapes your actions and your beliefs about the environment in which you operate. Without that knowledge you would think and act differently. So do your team.

🖎 Create insight into how systems form, decline, and reform. This is not a time for backward hunts; instead, encourage your team to consider different scenarios for the future – not just the elite few. Scout the competition and demonstrate concretely what alternatives look like.

🖎 Identify and overcome barriers. Name names. Initially people see these as external to themselves; 'It's their fault!' 'If it were not for management, we could . . .' Excuses and rationalization for removing barriers should be exposed.

🖎 Create the conditions for consolidation and support during transition. New ways of thinking need to germinate and bloom. Exciting discoveries have not yet become mature expressions and so may well appear clumsy and those who change may be punished. Sometimes, you will have to turn around and not look back. Holding the vision is key to the job of the team leader and it can be terrifying and lonely. If you are one, then make sure that you have a good coach or mentor to provide you with a wider viewpoint and keep you thinking straight.

Teams should develop a consistent and systemic approach to all the issues within the organizational loop – recruitment, selection, placement, training, internal management and external marketing – so they all align, integrate and synergize.

(A principle of Spiral Dynamics)

Progress now

1   Now you are ready to draw or paint your future picture of how you would like your life to be. When you have finished, date it. If possible, talk it through with a friend (a supporter, part of your Sangha – see Chapter 10).

2   Compare your picture of your future with the one you drew or painted at the beginning of the chapter: what differences do you notice?

3   Finally, ask yourself, 'What would have to be true in terms of my outer life and my inner team for me to have this life that I want?' and 'What two or three actions will move me towards it?'

SUMMARY

🖉 Use the future to imagine what life could be like for you.

🖉 Draw on feedback and advice from supporters and your inner champions.

🖉 Explore your core values: that which makes you tick and makes life fulfilling at all times.

🖉 Learn to be fast-paced in team skills and to operate skilfully within the many dimensions of future teams: be flexible when out of your comfort zone of knowledge, when diversity of culture, nationality and race require sensitivity to operate within other people's expectations, when global requirements mean using leverage and influence, and when virtual teams mean finding new ways of helping people feel that they belong.

🖉 When managing change within and across teams, be aware of whether people have their eyes closed to change, or perhaps feel blocked, or are open to change. Keep them informed of their environment, help them overcome barriers, and offer support during transition.

NOTES

NOTES

NOTES

NOTES